FINANCIAL INTELLIGENCE
FOR ENTREPRENEURS

FINANCIAL INTELLIGENCE

FOR ENTREPRENEURS

What You Really Need to Know About the Numbers

KAREN BERMAN

JOE KNIGHT

with John Case

HARVARD BUSINESS PRESS

BOSTON, MASSACHUSETTS

Library of Congress Cataloging-in-Publication Data
Berman, Karen, 1962–
    Financial intelligence for entrepreneurs : what you really need to know about the numbers / Karen Berman, Joe Knight; with John Case.
        p. cm.
    Includes bibliographical references and index.
    ISBN-978-1-4221-1915-0
    1. Financial statements. 2. Cash management. 3. Business enterprises—Finance. 4. Corporations—Finance. I. Knight, Joe, 1963– II. Case, John, 1944– III. Berman, Karen, 1962– Financial intelligence. IV. Title.
HG4028.B2B422   2008
658.15'11—dc22

                                                                        2008012635

Karen dedicates this book to
her husband, Young Riddle,
and their daughter, Marie.

Joe dedicates this book to his wife,
Donielle, and to the seven Js—
Jacob, Jordan, Jewel, Jessica, James, Jonah,
and Joseph Christian (JC).

CONTENTS

PART THREE

THE BALANCE SHEET REVEALS THE MOST

PART FOUR

CASH IS KING

PART EIGHT
CREATING A FINANCIALLY INTELLIGENT COMPANY

PREFACE

WHAT THIS BOOK IS ABOUT

This book is about financial intelligence—about knowing what the numbers really mean. It is written for entrepreneurs and company owners who need to understand exactly what is happening in their company from a financial perspective. It provides the financial knowledge you need to run your business more effectively.

In it, you'll learn how to read the three major financial statements and how to interpret the information they contain. You'll learn to calculate critical ratios and to understand what they are telling you. You'll learn why your net cash in a given time period is not the same thing as profit, and why you need *both* profit and cash. You'll learn to use return-on-investment (ROI) tools to analyze big purchases in order to make sure your investments add value to your business. You'll learn about managing working capital, which helps you improve your company's cash flow and profitability even with no change in sales or expenses. You'll read about the three main methods for establishing the value of your business and many other tricks of the financial trade.

Along the way, we'll let you in on the finance profession's little secret, which is that finance is as much art as it is science. Many of the numbers on a business's financial reports are determined by a whole series of estimates and assumptions. If you learn how to assess those estimates and assumptions, you will know how the reports you are seeing may be biased in one direction or another. Understanding the bias will help you make better decisions.

The original edition of this book was called just *Financial Intelligence*, and it was published by Harvard Business Press in 2006. It was designed primarily for nonfinancial managers in large corporations. Our company, the Business Literacy Institute (BLI), has taught the basics of finance to many thousands of leaders, managers, and employees in companies around the world.

But we noticed a funny thing. Many of our friends and acquaintances—entrepreneurs and business owners like ourselves—picked up copies of the book. They told us they found it helpful even though it wasn't really aimed at them. In some ways, we realized, we have more in common with these entrepreneurs than we do with the corporate managers who are our clients. Karen started BLI by herself, out of her home, right after earning her PhD in organizational psychology. Joe, who holds an MBA in finance, had worked at Ford Motor Company and several smaller businesses; then he joined two other guys named Joe in starting Setpoint, a company that manufactures roller coasters and factory-automation equipment. (At Setpoint, the trio is known as "the Joes.") Later, Joe joined Karen as co-owner of BLI.

We have both met a payroll. We know what it's like to start and run your own business. So we decided to work with Harvard Business Press to create the book you are holding, an edition of *Financial Intelligence* specially tailored for entrepreneurs and company owners. Let us tell you a little bit about this edition.

First, it contains all the meat of the original book. We have always tried to present financial material so that people who aren't familiar with the jargon can understand it, and we hope we have accomplished that goal in this book as well. But we didn't simplify or remove any of the concepts. This is the real stuff. When you have finished this book, you will know what your own company's income statement is telling you—and you will be able to read IBM's income statement, too. You will be able to talk numbers with bankers, prospective investors, and potential partners. You will be able to understand the financials of a company you may want to acquire, or one that may want to acquire yours. You will have the financial intelligence you need to manage your business as it grows.

Second, this book is for *all* entrepreneurs and company owners who want to build their business. If you're a financial novice, you won't find anything in here that is over your head. If you already know the basics of finance, you can use the book to review and refresh your understanding. Perhaps you are a so-called corporate entrepreneur, a manager who suddenly finds himself or herself heading a spin-off venture or a partnership with the parent corporation. If so, you will need to know the language of numbers not only to manage the business but also to communicate with the folks back at headquarters. Or maybe you operate a franchise business. This book will help you analyze your own franchise's financial performance compared to the performance of others and compared to the parent company's expectations.

Third, we're big believers in hands-on experience. In the back of the book, you'll find full financial statements for two publicly traded entrepreneurial companies. We have included some exercises that draw on these financials so you can practice working with the numbers. Of course, you can do the exercises using your own company's reports if you prefer. We hope you won't just read about finance; we hope you will roll up your sleeves and plunge in. That's the best way to learn.

There are some things we haven't tried to do in this book. For example, we don't teach accounting. We never mention debits and credits; we don't ever refer to the general ledger or trial balances. The book isn't another version of *Accounting for Dummies*. Nor will we advise you on how to finance your business, do your taxes, or buy financial software. There are plenty of good guidebooks to these subjects already on the shelves. Our subject is what you need to know about finance to run your business more effectively, and we try to stick to it.

Of course, learning about finance can get a little tedious at times. So we often illustrate our points with stories about the many financial frauds and scandals that came to light in the late 1990s and early 2000s. At first these may seem pretty far removed from the day-to-day experience of running a small company, but we left them in this edition for a reason. The principles that govern finance are the same in companies of every size. A big company called Waste Management, for example, at one point increased its profits enormously simply by changing how it depreciated its garbage trucks and other equipment. (We explain how it did that in chapter 6.) An entrepreneur applying for a loan might be tempted to try the same thing. It's good to be aware of how slippery some of these slopes can be. Besides, it's always entertaining to read about the bad guys.

In preparing this edition of our book, we interviewed a number of entrepreneurs to learn what their experience had been. Among them were Paul Saginaw and Ari Weinzweig, who hail from Ann Arbor, Michigan. Saginaw and Weinzweig founded the famous Zingerman's Deli because, as they tell it, they couldn't find a good corned-beef sandwich anywhere in town. They had some experience managing restaurants, but they didn't have any financial knowledge—Saginaw had been a biology major, while Weinzweig studied Russian history. Saginaw describes what it was like at first: "We didn't have a problem taking a lot of money in, but in the early going, we had a lot of trouble holding on to the money as it came in. The busier we got, the more money we lost." Maybe you recognize their plight. If so, this is the book for you.

We also spoke with Chip Conley, who started the San Francisco–based Joie de Vivre hotel chain when he was just twenty-six. Conley had a leg up on many entrepreneurs because he had studied finance at Stanford Graduate School of Business. But most of the other company owners he came to know were like Saginaw and Weinzweig: they tried to get by mostly on intuition and gut feel, and they ran into financial difficulties in the process.

According to Conley, "Operating by the seat of your pants is fine only if you've got some pretty thick pants. If you have thin pants, your rear end will be exposed pretty quickly."

We recommend building your financial intelligence rather than buying thicker pants.

Part One

The Art of Finance
(and Why It Matters)

1

What Is Financial Intelligence?

Since we teach finance for a living, we'll begin this book in the manner of teachers everywhere: by asking questions.

Do you know whether you will have enough cash to make payroll next month? How about the month after that?

If you're running a start-up, do you know your burn rate—that is, how fast you are going through your cash?

Do you know how profitable your company's products or services really are? Do you know that you can be running a profitable business and still run out of cash?

If you're thinking about buying a new piece of equipment—a truck, a computer system, a machine—do you know how to figure the likely return on your investment?

Many entrepreneurs can't answer yes to questions like these. The reason is that they haven't yet acquired the necessary financial intelligence.

Note that word: *acquired*. Financial intelligence, as we use the term, isn't some innate ability that you either have or don't have. Granted, some people are better at numbers than others, and a few legendary folks seem to have an intuitive grasp of finance that eludes everybody else. But that's not what we're talking about here. For most businesspeople—ourselves included—financial intelligence is simply a set of skills that can be learned.

People who work in finance pick up these skills early on and for the rest of their careers are able to talk with one another in a specialized language that can sound like Greek to the uninitiated. Most senior executives of large companies (not all) either come out of finance or learn the skills during their rise to the top, just because it's tough to run a big business unless you know what the financial folks are saying.

But how about you? Nobody gave you an exam in finance when you decided to start a business. You probably didn't launch your company just so that you could work with numbers. You may have had an accounting class in high school or college, but that isn't enough to prepare you to manage a business. So you may never have had the chance to pick up financial skills. But now is the time. You may be a great salesperson or an inspired engineer. You may be terrific with customers and employees. Your concept for a company is probably fantastic. But if you don't know finance, you're operating at a disadvantage in the world of business.

Fundamentally, financial intelligence boils down to three distinct skill sets. When you finish the book, you should be competent in all of them. Let's look at each one in turn.

UNDERSTANDING THE FOUNDATION

Not long ago, two acquaintances of ours were running their own business. They loved what they were doing. Their company seemed very successful—in fact, it was doubling its sales every year. The financial reports showed that the company was making money. At one point the entrepreneurs enthusiastically showed these reports to another friend, an experienced businessman, who perused them carefully.

Box Definitions

We want to make finance as easy as possible. Most finance books make us flip back and forth between the page we're on and the glossary to learn the definition of a word we don't know. By the time we find it and get back to our page, we've lost our train of thought. So here we are going to give you the definitions right where you need them, near the first time we use the word.

"I'm very afraid," he said, "that you will run out of cash in about eighteen months unless you take action now."

Frankly, the entrepreneurs didn't believe him. They wrote him off as a doomsayer. They knew their business was profitable, and they were certain that their hard work could overcome any obstacle.

You can probably see where we're going with this cautionary tale. Sure enough: in just about eighteen months, they called their friend to admit that they were maxed out on their credit cards and on the home-equity loans they had taken out on their houses. They had no more cash and no ability to borrow any more. The business was still booming. But if it was to survive, they would have to sell part of it to outside investors and themselves become minority shareholders.

Yet their friend had been able to see the problem coming *eighteen months ahead of time*, just because he was able to read the financial reports—the foundation of financial intelligence.

Some entrepreneurs think they don't need to bother with formal financial reports. They run the business out of their checkbook. Or maybe they get a bookkeeper to pay the bills and keep the records they need for taxes, but they don't really study the reports she prepares. That may be fine for one-person shops. But the minute your company begins to grow, as the owners of that ill-fated business discovered, you can no longer tell how it's doing financially just by looking at the checkbook. You need to see—and to understand—the information contained in the income statement, the balance sheet, and the cash flow statement. If you ever want a loan, moreover, or if you want to attract outside investors, your prospective lenders and shareholders will expect to see all these reports. And they will expect you to answer detailed questions about the data the reports contain.

Entrepreneurs who are financially intelligent understand these basics. They can read an income statement, a balance sheet, and a cash flow statement. They know the difference between profitability and a healthy cash flow. (As our story suggests, understanding cash is particularly important to entrepreneurs.) They understand why the balance sheet balances. The numbers neither scare nor mystify them.

We'll consider the three main financial reports in parts 2, 3, and 4 of the book—and we'll answer questions such as why profit isn't the same as cash.

Income Statement

The income statement shows revenues, expenses, and profit for a period of time, such as a month, quarter, or year. It's also called a profit and loss statement, P&L, statement of earnings, or statement of operations. Big companies sometimes throw the word *consolidated* in front of those phrases, but it's still just an income statement. The bottom line of the income statement is net profit, also known as net income or net earnings. We explain the income statement in part 2.

UNDERSTANDING THE ART OF FINANCE

A second aspect of financial intelligence is understanding what might be called the art of finance. In the preface we referred to it as the finance profession's little secret, but it isn't really a secret; it's a widely acknowledged truth that everyone who has studied finance knows. Trouble is, the rest of us tend to forget it. We think that if a number shows up on a financial statement or on your accountants' reports, it must accurately represent reality.

Of course, that can't always be true, if only because bookkeepers and accountants can't know everything. They can't know exactly what everyone in the company does every day, so they don't know exactly how to allocate costs. They can't know exactly how long a piece of equipment will last, so they don't know how much of its original cost to record in any given year. The art of accounting and finance is the art of using limited data to come as close as possible to an accurate description of how well a company is performing. Accounting and finance are not reality; they are a reflection of reality, and the accuracy of that reflection depends on the ability of bookkeepers, accountants, and finance professionals to make reasonable assumptions and to calculate reasonable estimates.

It's a tough job. Sometimes the accountants and finance folks have to quantify what can't easily be quantified. Sometimes they have to make difficult judgments about how to categorize a given item. None of these complications necessarily arises because they are trying to cook the books or because they are incompetent. The complications arise because they must make educated guesses relating to the numbers side of the business all day long.

Balance Sheet

The balance sheet reflects the assets, liabilities, and owners' equity at a point in time. In other words, it shows, on a specific day, what the company owned, what it owed, and how much it was worth. The balance sheet is called such because it balances—assets always must equal liabilities plus owners' equity. A financially savvy entrepreneur knows that all the financial statements ultimately flow to the balance sheet. Part 3 takes up the balance sheet.

The result of these assumptions and estimates is, typically, a bias in the numbers. Please don't get the idea that by using the word *bias* we are impugning anybody's integrity. (Some of our best friends are accountants—no, really—and one of us, Joe, actually carries the title CFO on his business card.) Where financial results are concerned, bias means only that the numbers might be skewed in one direction or another. It means only that bookkeepers, accountants, and finance professionals have used certain assumptions and estimates rather than others when they put their reports together. Enabling you to understand this bias, to correct for it where necessary, and even to use it to your company's advantage is one objective of this book.

So financially intelligent entrepreneurs are able to identify where the artful aspects of finance have been applied to the numbers, and they know how applying them differently might lead to different conclusions. They are prepared, when appropriate, to question and challenge the numbers they get from their accountants or finance folks. In the following chapter we'll show you some specific examples of the art of finance, but it's a lesson you'll want to bear in mind throughout the book.

UNDERSTANDING FINANCIAL ANALYSIS

Once you can read the financials, and once you have an appreciation of the art of finance, you can use the information to analyze the numbers in greater depth and to make decisions based on what you learn. For example, did you know the following?

- A couple of simple ratios derived from the balance sheet will tell you at a glance whether you're going to be able to pay your bills during the coming year. If you can't pay your bills, you may decide to apply for a loan. These are the same ratios bankers will use to make an initial judgment about whether they should consider your company creditworthy.

- Profitability ratios—derived from the income statement—help you understand how much money your company is making. If your goal is to maximize profits, you want these ratios to be as high as possible. But there's one profitability ratio that can be *too* high. If it's higher than your competitors', or higher than industry averages, it may be a sign that you are failing to manage your business as well as you could.

- Efficiency ratios, as they are known, tell you how well you are managing the assets that you are putting to work in your company. Once you understand these ratios, you will know how to improve your company's profits and cash flow *without any change in sales or costs*.

Financially intelligent entrepreneurs learn to understand and analyze many such ratios. They use their analyses to inform their decisions, and they make better decisions for doing so. Over time, they watch trends in the critical ratios to make sure they're on the right track. That skill, by the way, is one key to the story about the entrepreneurs who ran out of cash. The entrepreneurs' friend could see from the trend line in a couple of critical ratios that the business would run out of cash in about eighteen months.

Financially intelligent entrepreneurs also know how to do return-on-investment (ROI) calculations. Before they buy a new truck, computer, or

Cash (and Cash Flow Statement)

Cash means the money a company has in the bank, plus anything else (like stocks and bonds) that can readily be turned into cash. Really, it is that simple. The cash flow statement shows cash coming in, cash going out, and the difference between them. We'll talk about cash and describe the cash flow statement in part 4.

piece of machinery, they analyze the numbers to see whether the purchase is worth it. We'll take up ratios and ROI in parts 5 and 6 of this book, and we'll have more to say on that business of improving your profits and cash flow without changing sales or costs in part 7.

So those are the key elements of financial intelligence and the key elements of what you will learn in the book. These elements are what you need to know about finance. Familiarize yourself with them, and you will be a better—a financially intelligent—businessperson.

ROADBLOCKS TO FINANCIAL INTELLIGENCE

We have worked with enough people and companies to know that while everyone might want to increase his or her financial intelligence, it isn't always easy. In fact, we run into several predictable obstacles.

One obstacle might be that you hate math, fear math, and don't want to do math. You started a company—or you're thinking about starting one—because you had a new idea or because you wanted to be your own boss. You aren't necessarily a fan of numbers.

Well, join the club. It might surprise you to know that, for the most part, finance involves addition and subtraction. When finance people get really fancy, they multiply and divide. You will never have to take the second derivative of a function or determine the area under a curve (sorry, engineers). So have no fear: the math is easy, and calculators are cheap. You don't need to be a rocket scientist to be financially intelligent.

A second possible obstacle is your feeling that, on some level, profit isn't your real objective. Perhaps your primary goal is to satisfy customers, help support your community, or provide incredible service. We have two responses to this concern. One is that if you don't make a profit, you won't have a business at all. Profit gives you the resources you need to keep the business going day to day (and year to year). Profit helps you finance growth. Profit ensures that your business continues so that you can keep on satisfying customers, supporting your community, and providing incredible service. (If you are running a nonprofit, the same concept applies: even nonprofits need to have funds left over after they pay all the bills.) Our second response is simply to note that you are the owner or one of the owners of this business. You've probably invested your own money in it.

You could have invested in something else, and you would probably have earned some sort of return on your investment. So you should expect that, eventually, you'll get a return on the money that you put into *this* investment. That return comes when the company makes a profit.

A third possibility is that you're afraid of appearing ignorant. You want your accountant, banker, and other financial advisers to think that you understand everything they tell you, even when you don't. Well, reading this book will enable you to ask intelligent questions and to decipher their answers. Asking questions, as PBS Kids tells our children, is a good way to find things out.

A fourth possibility: you don't have time. Just give us enough time to read the book. If you fly for business, take it with you on a trip or two. In just a few hours, you will become a lot more knowledgeable about finance than you have ever been in the past. Alternatively, keep it somewhere handy. The chapters are deliberately short, and you can read one whenever you have a few spare moments. What could be more fun than reading a bit about the balance sheet on the beach during your next vacation?

If you can overcome these obstacles, you will have a healthy appreciation of the art of finance, and you will increase your financial intelligence. You won't magically acquire an MBA in finance, but you will be an appreciative consumer of the numbers, someone who's capable of understanding and assessing what the financial reports are saying and asking appropriate questions about them. The numbers will no longer scare you.

One final caution before we move on. Although we teach finance, and although we think that every entrepreneur should understand the numbers side of his or her business, we are equally firm in our belief that numbers can't and don't tell the whole story. A business's financial results must always be understood in context—that is, within the framework of the big picture. Factors such as the economy, the competitive environment, regulations, changing customer needs and expectations, and new technologies all affect how you should interpret the numbers and what decisions you should make. Numbers should inform your decisions, not determine what you decide.

2

A Primer on the Art of Finance

In the following chapter we're going to plunge into the first of the three major financial statements. But before we do, we want to tell you a little more about that secret in accounting. We've already warned you that many of the numbers aren't real in the same sense as your bank balance is real. Rather, they are based on estimates and assumptions—on the art of finance. In this chapter we want to help you understand what to look for.

If you're like a lot of entrepreneurs, you may be a little mystified by the idea that finance is partly an art. Everything else in the business world—marketing, operations, managing people, and so on—is obviously subjective, a matter dependent on experience and judgment as well as data. But finance? Accounting? Surely, the numbers produced by the accountants are objective, black and white, indisputable. Surely, a company sold what it sold, spent what it spent, earned what it earned.

The best way to understand why this isn't so is to look at specific examples.

One of the variables that is frequently estimated, for instance, is *revenue* or *sales*—that is, the value of what a company sold to its customers during a given period. You'd think revenue would be an easy matter to determine. But the question is when revenue should be recorded (or "recognized," as accountants like to say). Here are some possibilities:

- When a contract is signed

- When the product or service is delivered

- When the invoice is sent out

- When the bill is paid

If you said, "When the product or service is delivered," you're correct, as long as you are using accrual accounting (more on this in chapter 3). As we'll see in chapter 5, that's the fundamental rule that determines when a sale should show up on the income statement. Still, the rule isn't simple. Implementing it requires making a number of assumptions. In fact, the whole question of "when is a sale a sale?" was a hot topic in many of the fraud cases dating from the late 1990s.

Imagine, for instance, that you run a business that resells specialized telephone equipment to local customers. Most of your customers buy the equipment with a maintenance contract, and the whole thing is wrapped up in one financial package. Now, suppose you deliver the equipment in October, but the maintenance contract is good for the following twelve months. How much of the initial purchase price should be recorded on the books for October? After all, you haven't yet delivered all the services that you are responsible for during the year. Your accountant can estimate the value of those services, of course, and adjust the revenue for October accordingly. But this requires a big judgment call.

This example isn't purely hypothetical. Witness Xerox, which played a game with revenue recognition on such a massive scale that it was later found to have improperly recognized a whopping $6 billion of sales. The issue? Xerox was selling equipment on four-year contracts, including service and maintenance. So how much of the price covered the cost of the equipment, and how much was for the subsequent services? Fearful that the company's sagging profits would cause its stock price to plummet, Xerox's executives decided to book ever-increasing percentages of the anticipated revenues—along with the associated profits—up front. Before long, nearly all the revenue on these contracts was being recognized at the time of the sale.

Xerox had clearly lost its way and was trying to use accounting to cover up its business failings. But you can see the point here: there's plenty of

Operating Expenses

Operating expenses are the costs that are required to keep a business going day to day. They include salaries, benefits, and insurance costs, among a host of other items. Operating expenses appear on the income statement.

room, short of outright book-cooking, to make the numbers look one way or another.

A second example of the artful work of finance—and another one that played a huge role in the financial scandals that came to light in the late 1990s and 2000s—is determining whether a given cost is a capital expenditure or an operating expense. We'll get to all the details later; for the moment, all you need to know is that an operating expense reduces profit immediately and that a capital expenditure spreads the hit over several accounting periods. You can see the temptation here. *Wait. You mean if we take all those office supply purchases and call them capital expenditures, we can make ourselves look a lot more profitable?* This is the kind of thinking that got WorldCom, for example, into trouble (more on WorldCom later in the book). To prevent such temptation, both the accounting profession and individual companies have rules about what must be classified where. But the rules leave a good deal up to individual judgment and discretion. Again, those judgments can affect a company's profit dramatically. If it's a public company, they'll affect its stock price as well. If it's a small business, judgments that are too close to the line may make the bankers nervous.

You need to know about such judgment calls because you use numbers to make decisions. No matter what your definition of success is—business excellence, professional achievement, personal satisfaction, financial rewards, or some combination—the numbers tell you what is going on in your business and where you need to focus your attention. You make decisions about budgets, capital expenditures, staffing, and a dozen other matters based on an assessment of your company's financial situation. If you aren't aware of the assumptions and estimates that underlie the numbers and how those assumptions and estimates affect the numbers in one direction or another, your decisions may be faulty.

Capital Expenditures

A capital expenditure is the purchase of an item that's considered a long-term investment, such as computer systems and equipment. Most companies follow the rule that any purchase over a certain dollar amount counts as a capital expenditure, while anything less is an operating expense. Operating expenses show up on the income statement and thus reduce profit. Capital expenditures show up on the balance sheet; only the depreciation of a piece of capital equipment appears on the income statement. More on this in chapters 3 and 9.

Financial intelligence in this context means understanding where the numbers are "hard" (that is, well supported and relatively uncontroversial) and where they are "soft" (that is, highly dependent on those judgment calls). What's more, your investors, bankers, vendors, and maybe even your customers will be using your company's numbers as a basis for their own decisions. If you don't have a good working understanding of the financial statements and don't know what those folks are looking at or why, you are at their mercy.

So let's plunge a little deeper into this element of financial intelligence, understanding the artistic aspects of finance. We'll look at two examples and ask where the assumptions and estimates are and what they might mean. The examples we'll look at are depreciation and valuation. If these words

Depreciation

Depreciation allows accountants to spread the cost of equipment and other assets over more than one accounting period. Most capital expenditures are depreciated (land is an example of one that isn't). Accountants attempt to depreciate the item over what they believe will be its useful life. There's more about depreciation in parts 2 and 3.

sound like part of that strange language the financial folks speak, don't worry. You'll be surprised how quickly you can pick up enough to get around.

DISCRETION ABOUT DEPRECIATION

The notion of depreciation isn't complicated. Say your company buys a computer system or truck that it expects to use for several years. Accountants think about such an event like this: rather than subtract the entire cost from one month's revenues—perhaps plunging the company into the red for that month—we should spread the cost out over the equipment's useful life. If we think a truck will last three years, for instance, we can record ("depreciate") one-third of the cost per year, or one-thirty-sixth per month, using a simple straight-line method of depreciation. That's a better way of estimating the company's true costs in any given month or year than if we recorded it all at once. Furthermore, it better matches the cost of the equipment to the revenue that it is used to generate—an important idea that we will explore at length in chapter 3.

The theory makes perfect sense. In practice, however, accountants have a good deal of discretion about exactly how a piece of equipment is depreciated. And that discretion can have a considerable impact. Take the airline industry. Some years back, airlines realized that their planes were lasting longer than anticipated. So the industry's accountants changed their depreciation schedules to reflect that longer life. As a result, they subtracted less depreciation from revenue each month. And guess what? The industry's profits rose significantly, reflecting the fact that the airlines wouldn't have to be buying replacement planes as soon as they had thought. But note that the accountants had to assume that they could predict how long a plane would be useful. On that judgment—and a judgment it is—hung the resulting upward bias in the profit numbers. On that judgment, too, hung all the implications: investors deciding to buy more stock, airline executives figuring they could afford to give out better raises, and so on.

If your business owns any significant tangible assets, you should understand how your accountants depreciate them. The accountants' practices will go far toward determining your company's bottom line. You are using that bottom-line number to make decisions about what the business can and should do next. And you can bet your banker will want to know the details of depreciation if you ever apply for a loan.

THE MANY METHODS OF VALUATION

Another example of the art of finance has to do with the valuation of a company—that is, figuring out how much a company is worth. Publicly traded companies, of course, are valued every day by the stock market. They are worth whatever their stock price is multiplied by the number of shares outstanding, a figure known as their market capitalization or just market cap. But even that doesn't necessarily capture their value in certain circumstances. A competitor bent on a takeover, for instance, might decide to pay a premium for the company's shares because the target company is worth more to that competitor than it is on the open market.

The millions of companies that are privately held, of course, aren't valued at all on the market. When they are bought or sold, the buyers and sellers must rely on other methods of valuation. Talk about the art of finance: much of the art here lies in choosing the valuation method. Different methods produce different results—which, of course, injects a bias into the numbers.

Suppose, for example, you run a small chain of restaurants. How much is it worth?

Well, you could look at your company's earnings (another word for profits) and then see how the stock market values large restaurant chains in relation to their earnings. (This is known as the price-to-earnings ratio method.) Or you could look at how much cash your restaurants generate each year and figure that a buyer, in effect, would be buying that stream of cash. Then you would use some interest rate to determine what that stream of future cash is worth today. (This is the discounted cash flow method.) Alternatively, you could simply look at your company's assets—its real estate, equipment, inventory, and so on, along with intangibles such as its reputation and customer list—and make estimates about what those assets are worth (the asset valuation method).

Needless to say, each method entails a whole passel of assumptions and estimates. The price-to-earnings method, for example, assumes that the stock market is somehow rational and that the prices it sets are therefore accurate. (It also assumes that the prices are applicable to privately held companies.) But the stock market reflects many factors other than the outlook for any one business. If investors are bullish (optimistic) on the future, for example, the market will be high, and your company will be valued at more than it would be if investors were feeling bearish (pessimistic) and the market were low. And besides, that earnings number, as we'll see in part 2, is itself an estimate.

So maybe, you might think, we should use the discounted cash flow method. The question with this method is, what is the right interest or discount rate to use when we're calculating the value of that stream of cash (which is itself an estimate)? Depending on how we set the rate, the value of your business could vary enormously. And of course, the asset valuation method itself is merely a collection of guesses about what each asset might be worth.

As if these uncertainties weren't enough, think back to that delightful, outrageous, nerve-racking period known as the dot-com boom, at the end of the twentieth century. Ambitious young Internet companies were springing up all over, fed and watered by a torrent of enthusiastic venture capital. But when investors such as venture capitalists (VCs) put their money into something, they like to know what their investment—and hence what the company—is worth. When a company is just starting up, that's tough to know. Profits? Zero. Operating cash flow? Also zero. Assets? Negligible. In ordinary times, that's one reason VCs shy away from early-stage investments. But in the dot-com era, they were throwing caution to the wind and so were relying on what we can only call unusual methods of valuation. They looked at the number of engineers on a company's payroll. They counted the number of hits ("eyeballs") a company got every month on its Web site. One energetic young CEO of our acquaintance raised millions of dollars based almost entirely on the fact that he had hired a large staff of software engineers. Unfortunately, we observed a "For Lease" sign in front of this company's office less than a year later.

The dot-com methods of valuation look foolish now, even though they didn't seem so bad back then, given how little we knew about what the future held. But the other methods described earlier are all reasonable. Trouble is, each has a bias that leads to different results. And the implications are far reaching. Companies like your own are bought and sold based on these valuations. They get loans based on them. The equity you hold in your company should reflect an appropriate valuation, and when the time comes to sell your business, the buyer will probably use some combination of these methods to determine what he or she offers. It seems reasonable to us that your financial intelligence should include an understanding of how those numbers are calculated.

So keep the art of finance in mind as we proceed through the rest of the book. As we'll see, it crops up repeatedly.

Part One
TOOLBOX

FINANCING YOUR BUSINESS

The financing of most entrepreneurial companies begins with the owner's checkbook and credit cards. "One definition of a small business is that if you have never put a payroll on your Visa, you're not a small business," says Ed Zimmer, CEO of ECCO, a Boise, Idaho, manufacturer of lighting, alarm, and other safety-related products. Some entrepreneurial companies continue to work on that basis. But most soon establish a business checking account, keep regular books (using QuickBooks or other accounting software), and hire a bookkeeper. At some point along the way, many entrepreneurial companies look for additional funds to finance their operations and growth. There are three generic sources of financing:

- *Owner financing.* Entrepreneurs often put a lot of their own money into their businesses. They draw down their savings accounts. They take a second mortgage out on their houses. Their contributions of cash can be structured as equity investments in the business or as loans from the entrepreneur to the business. You should get an accountant or financial adviser to help you figure out the best way to structure the financing, taking into account taxes, future banking and financing requirements, and other considerations.

- *Other equity investment.* If you get friends, family, or so-called angel investors to put money into the business, they will expect shares of stock in return. That is, they will be co-owners of the business with you. If their investment is large enough, they may be entitled to a seat on the board of directors, a say in major decisions, or both. They are your de facto business partners and shoulder part of the risk of the business. If you succeed, their stock will grow in value. If you fail, they may lose their investment.

- *Debt.* Of course, you can also ask for loans from friends and family, or from your local bank. Banks won't normally lend money to start-up businesses, but they will often lend to a start-up entrepreneur *provided* that the entrepreneur's personal finances are healthy enough to ensure repayment of the loan whatever the fate of the business. People who lend you money are not part owners of the business and aren't entitled to a say in major decisions. But you do have to pay them back on the agreed-upon terms. If you fail to do so, they are likely to have a legal claim on your assets.

BUILDING A FINANCIAL STAFF

An entrepreneurial company typically starts out with one person on the financial staff: a part-time bookkeeper (who may be the entrepreneur himself or herself, or a spouse). As your company grows, you may need a full-time bookkeeper (or bookkeeping firm), and you will also need an accountant, who can review your financial statements and prepare tax returns. For many companies, that's enough—particularly if your accountant is also qualified to serve as a financial adviser. "In my company, it was not until year three that I had internal accounting people," says Chip Conley, CEO of Joie de Vivre Hospitality, a San Francisco–based hotel company that now has nearly $200 million in revenues. "For two years it was just outsourcing."

But if and when your company grows significantly bigger, you will have to add full-time financial staff. Here's a guide to the different titles and what they're responsible for in larger companies:

- *Chief financial officer.* CFOs in many companies are in charge of other internal departments as well, such as human resources and information technology. But their chief job is to oversee the management and strategy of the organization from a financial perspective. They are ultimately responsible for all the financial functions. In an entrepreneurial company, it is typically the CFO who plays the leading role in lining up financing, negotiating and structuring loans, managing cash flow, and making decisions about the company's capital structure. The CFO is also ultimately responsible for the quality of the financial reporting. And he or she should use that information to advise you on the financial issues facing the company.

- *Treasurer.* In larger companies, the treasurer is the financial person who deals with the outside world—meeting with analysts (for public companies), communicating with investors, and negotiating with bankers. Some would say that the ideal treasurer is a finance professional with a personality. The treasurer reports to the CFO.

- *Controller.* Again, this is a separate position only in larger companies. The focus of the controller—sometimes spelled *comptroller*—is purely internal. His or her job is providing reliable and accurate financial reports. The controller is responsible for general accounting, financial reporting, business analysis, financial planning, asset management, and internal controls. He or she ensures that day-to-day transactions are recorded accurately and correctly. Without good, consistent data from the controller, the CFO and the treasurer can't do their jobs.

The (Many) Peculiarities of the Income Statement

3

Profit Is an Estimate

In a familiar phrase generally attributed to Peter Drucker, profit is the sovereign criterion of the enterprise. The use of the word *sovereign* is right on the money. A profitable company charts its own course. If your company is profitable, you can run it the way you want to. When a company stops being profitable, other people—lenders, outside investors, suppliers, even customers—begin to poke their noses into the business. The company loses its autonomy.

Another familiar saying, this one attributed to Laurence J. Peter of *The Peter Principle*, tells us that if we don't know where we're going, we'll probably end up somewhere else. If you don't know how to make your company profitable, you're unlikely to succeed in doing so.

In fact, too many entrepreneurs don't understand what profit really is, let alone how it is calculated. Nor do they understand that a company's profit in any given period reflects a whole host of estimates and assumptions. The art of finance might just as easily be termed the art of making a profit.

We'll focus first on understanding an income statement because "profit" is no more and no less than what shows up there. Learn to decipher this document, and you will be able to understand and evaluate your company's profitability better than you could before. Learn to manage some of the key lines on the income statement, and you will make your company more profitable than before. Learn the art involved in determining profit, and you will definitely increase your financial intelligence. You might even get where you are going.

A (VERY) LITTLE ACCOUNTING

We told you early on that we wouldn't teach you accounting, and so we won't. There is one accounting concept, however, that we will explain to you in this chapter, because once you understand it, you will grasp exactly what the income statement is and what it is trying to tell you. First, though, we want to back up one step and make sure there isn't a major misconception lurking in your mind.

You know that the income statement is supposed to show a company's profit for a given period—usually a month, a quarter, or a year. It's only a short leap of imagination to conclude that the income statement shows how much cash the company took in during that period, how much it spent, and how much was left over. That leftover amount would then be the company's profit, right?

Alas, no. To be sure, some small businesses do their accounting this way. It's called cash-based accounting, and maybe that's how you kept your books when your business was just starting up. You take in money, and you record a sale. You pay a bill, and you record an expense. For a one-person shop or a small retail store, cash-based accounting may be sufficient.

But just about every company in the world other than the smallest (or newest) uses what's known as accrual accounting—and in accrual accounting, an income statement measures something quite different from cash in the door, cash out the door, and cash left over. It measures *sales* or *revenues*, *costs* or *expenses*, and *profit* or *income*.

Any income statement begins with sales. When a business delivers a product or a service to a customer, accountants say it has made a sale. Never mind if the customer hasn't paid for the product or service yet—the business may count the amount of the sale on the top line of its income statement for the period in question. No money at all may have changed hands. Of course, for cash-based businesses such as retailers and restaurants, sales and cash coming in are pretty much the same. But most businesses have to wait thirty days or more to collect on their sales.

And the "cost" lines of the income statement? In accrual accounting, the costs and expenses a company reports in any given period are not necessarily the ones it wrote checks for during that period. *The costs and ex-*

The Matching Principle

The matching principle is a fundamental accounting rule for preparing an income statement. It simply states, "Match the costs with the associated sale to determine profits in a given period of time—usually a month, quarter, or year." In other words, one of the accountants' primary jobs is to figure out and properly record all the costs incurred in generating sales.

penses on the income statement are those it incurred in generating the sales recorded during the time period. Accountants call this the *matching principle*—that appropriate costs should be *matched* to the sales for the period represented in the income statement—and it's the key to understanding how profit is determined.

The matching principle is the little bit of accounting you need to learn. For example:

- If an ink-and-toner company buys a truckload of cartridges in June to resell to customers over the next several months, it does not record the cost of all those cartridges in June. Rather, it records the cost of each cartridge when the cartridge is sold. The reason is the matching principle.

- And if a delivery company buys a truck in January that it plans to use over the next three years, the cost of the truck doesn't show up on the income statement for January. Rather, the truck is depreciated over the whole three years, with one-thirty-sixth of the truck's cost appearing as an expense on the income statement each month (assuming a simple straight-line method of depreciation). Why? The matching principle. The truck is one of the many costs associated with each month's work.

- The matching principle even extends to items like taxes. Your company may pay its tax bill once a quarter—but every month your accountant will tuck into the income statement a figure reflecting the taxes owed on that month's profits.

• The matching principle applies to service companies as well as product companies. A consulting firm, for example, sells billable hours, which refer to the time each consultant spends working with a client. Accountants still need to match the expenses associated with the time—consultant costs, materials costs, research costs, and so on—to the revenue that is generated.

You can see how far we are from cash in and cash out. Tracking the flow of cash in and out the door is the job of another financial document, namely the cash flow statement (part 4). You can also see how far we are from simple objective reality. Accountants can't just tote up the flow of dollars; they have to *decide* which costs are associated with the sales. They have to make assumptions and come up with estimates. In the process, they may introduce bias into the numbers.

Why go to so much trouble? Wouldn't it be easier just to stick with cash-based accounting? It would indeed be easier, but for most companies cash-based accounting wouldn't give an accurate picture of reality. That ink-and-toner company, for instance, might record a huge loss in the month when it paid for the truckload of cartridges and correspondingly higher profit in the other months. The owner of the business might know the reason, but nobody else looking at the company's income statement would understand why the bottom line was bouncing around so much. As the business grew—as it added other locations, for instance—even the owner might not understand what caused the volatility. Accrual accounting matches costs to sales, so it gives you a more accurate picture of whether you're really making money on your sales.

THE PURPOSE OF THE INCOME STATEMENT

In other words, the income statement tries to measure whether the products or services that a company provides are profitable when everything is added up. It's the accountants' best effort to show the sales the company generated during a given time period, the costs incurred in making those sales (including the costs of operating the business for that span of time), and the profit, if any, that is left over. Possible bias aside, this is a critically important endeavor for any company owner. If your company is big enough to have a management team, it's equally important for the members of that team. Your sales manager needs to know what kind of profits she and her group are generating so that she can make decisions about discounts, terms, which customers to pursue, and so on. Your marketing manager needs to know which products are most profitable so that those can be emphasized in marketing campaigns. Your human resource manager should know the profitability of products so that he knows where the company's strategic priorities are likely to lie when he is recruiting new people.

At the same time, however, an entrepreneurial company can't rely on profitability alone. Since profit is an estimate, a company can be profitable and still run out of cash—just as the company that we described in chapter 1 did.

Here's why. Profit is based on revenue. Revenue, remember, is recognized when a product or service is delivered, not when the bill is paid. So the top line of the income statement, the line from which we subtract expenses to determine profit, is often no more than a promise. Customers have not paid yet, so the revenue number does not reflect real money and neither does the profit line at the bottom. You can be making money as shown by the income statement, but you may not be generating cash fast enough to pay your bills.

Say you are running a fast-growing business-services company. The company is selling a lot of services at a good price; its revenues and profits are high. It is hiring people as fast as it can, and of course it has to pay them as soon as they come on board. But all the profit that these people are earning won't turn into cash until thirty days or maybe sixty days after it is billed out! That's one reason why even a highly profitable company may find that cash is tight. And it's one reason why many entrepreneurial businesses run out of cash.

Over time, the income statement and the cash flow statement in a well-run company will track one another. *Profit* will be turned into *cash.* As we saw in chapter 1, however, just because a company is making a profit in any given time period doesn't mean it will have the cash to pay its bills. Profit is always an estimate—and you can't spend estimates.

With that lesson under our belts, let's turn to the business of decoding the income statement.

Cracking the Code of
the Income Statement

Note the word we used in the title to this chapter: *code.* Unfortunately, an income statement can often seem like a code that needs to be deciphered.

Here's the reason. In books like this one—and even later in this book—you will often find cute little sample income statements. They look something like this:

Revenue	$100
Cost of goods sold	50
Gross profit	50
Expenses	30
Taxes	5
Net profit	$ 15

A bright fourth grader wouldn't need much help figuring out that one, once she had a little help with definitions. She could even do the math without a calculator. But now check out a real-world income statement, like your own company's. It's likely to have dozens of lines, and you may wonder what each one includes. If you were looking at a detailed statement for a midsize or large company, it could go on for pages—line after line after line of numbers, usually in print so small you can barely read it. Even if it's a "consolidated" statement like those you find in the annual reports of publicly traded corporations, it may contain at least a few lines with arcane labels like "conversion of subordinated debentures" (that's from Johnson & Johnson). It's enough to make anybody but a financial professional throw up his hands in dismay.

In this part we'll help you understand the income statement's secrets. And although your company isn't a Johnson & Johnson, we'll run through the whole drill, just as we promised; you will be able to decipher their income statements as well as your own. But mostly, we want to show you how the income statement can help you understand what is going on in your company and how to use that information to make decisions and lead your organization.

We'll start by mentioning some simple procedures for curling up with an income statement. Boosting your financial intelligence shouldn't involve an attack of heartburn, and learning these steps may save you from just that.

READING AN INCOME STATEMENT

Before you even start contemplating the numbers, you need some context for understanding the document.

The Label

Accountants put labels at the top of every report they give you. Does the document say "income statement"? It may not. It may instead say "profit and loss statement" or "P&L statement," "operating statement" or "statement of operations," "statement of earnings" or "earnings statement." Companies of all sizes use different language. We work with a client that calls the income statement in its annual report a statement of earnings. Meanwhile, one of the company's major divisions calls its income statement an income statement—and another major division calls it a profit and loss statement! With all these terms for the same thing, one might get the idea that our friends in finance and accounting don't want us to know what is going on. Or maybe they just take it for granted that everybody knows that all these different terms mean the same thing. However that may be, in this book we will always use the term *income statement*.

Incidentally, if you see "balance sheet" or "statement of cash flows" at the top, you have the wrong document. The label pretty much has to include one of those phrases we just mentioned.

What It's Measuring

If this is your own company's income statement, it's obviously for the entire business. If you were running a division of a large company, you might see income statements for the whole company, your division, its business units, maybe even its regions. H. Thomas Johnson and Robert S. Kaplan, in their classic book *Relevance Lost*, tell how General Motors developed the divisional system—with income statements for each division—in the first half of the twentieth century.[1] Corporate managers are glad it did. Creating income statements for smaller business units has provided them with enormous insights into their financial performance. If your company has more than one store, plant, or branch office, you may want to see income statements for each one.

Next, check the time period. An income statement, like a report card in school, is always for a span of time: a month, quarter, year, or maybe year-to-date. Some companies produce income statements for a time span as short as a week. Now consider how the numbers are actually presented. Your own company's figures are likely to be given just as they are: in thousands or millions. Big companies, however, usually omit the last zeros. So if you're looking at one of their income statements, look for a little note at the top: "in thousands" (add three zeros to the numbers) or "in millions" (add six zeros). This may sound like common sense, but we have found that seemingly trivial details such as this one are often overlooked by financial newcomers.

"Actual" Versus "Pro Forma"

Your company's income statement is *actual*: it shows what "actually" happened to revenues, costs, and profits during that time period according to the rules of accounting. (We put "actually" in quotes to remind you that *any* income statement has those built-in estimates, assumptions, and biases, which we will discuss in more detail later in this part of the book.)

But there are also *pro forma* income statements, as they are known. Sometimes pro forma means that the income statement is a projection. If you are drawing up a plan for a new business, for instance, you might come up with a projected income statement for the first year or two—in other words, what you hope and expect will happen in terms of sales and costs. That projection is called a pro forma. But pro forma can also mean an income statement that excludes any unusual or one-time charges. Say you're looking at the income statement of a company you're thinking about acquiring. Now suppose that this company had to take a big write-off in a particular year, resulting in a loss on the bottom line. (More on write-offs later in this part.) Along with its actual income statement, it might prepare one that shows what would have happened without the write-off.

Be careful with this kind of pro forma! Its ostensible purpose is to let you compare last year (when there was no write-off) with this year (if there hadn't been that ugly write-off). But there is often a subliminal message, something along the lines of, "Hey, things aren't really as bad as they look—we just lost money because of that write-off." Of course, the write-off really did happen, and the company really did lose money. Most of the time, you want to look at the actuals as well as the pro formas, and if you have to choose just one, the actuals are probably the better bet. Cynics sometimes describe pro formas as income statements with all the bad stuff taken out, which is how it sometimes appears.

The Big Numbers

No matter whose income statement you're looking at, there will be three main categories. One is *sales*, which may be called *revenue* (it's the same thing). Sales or revenue is always at the top. When people refer to top-line growth, that's what they mean: sales growth. Costs and expenses are in the middle, and profit is at the bottom. (If the income statement you're looking at is for a nonprofit, "profit" may be called "surplus/deficit" or "net revenue.") There are subsets of profit that may be listed as you go along, too—gross profit, for example. We'll explain the different forms of profit in chapter 7.

You can usually tell what's important to a company—your own or any other—by looking at the biggest numbers relative to sales. For example, the "sales" line is usually followed by "cost of goods sold," or COGS. In a service business, the line is often "cost of services," or COS. If that line is a large fraction of sales, chances are you'll want to watch COGS or COS very closely. But you better know exactly what goes into it. As we'll see, accountants have some discretion about how they categorize various expenses.

(By the way, unless you're a financial professional, you can usually ignore items like "conversion of subordinated debentures," should you ever come across them on a public company's income statement. Most lines with labels like that aren't material to the bottom line anyway. And if they are, they ought to be explained in the footnotes.)

Comparative Data

The consolidated income statements presented in public companies' annual reports typically have three columns of figures, reflecting what happened during the past three years. Income statements prepared for internal use—your own—may have many more columns. Maybe your bookkeeper or accountant gives you something like this, for example:

Actual % of sales   Budget % of sales   Variance %

Or like this:

Actual previous period $ Change (+/–)   % Change

These are pretty straightforward. In the first case, "% of sales" is simply a way of showing the magnitude of an expense number relative to revenue. The revenue line is taken as a given—a fixed point—and everything else is compared with it. Many companies set percent-of-sales targets for given line items and then take action if they miss the target by a significant amount. For instance, you might decide that selling expenses shouldn't be more than 12 percent of sales. If the number creeps up much above 12 percent, you'll want the sales manager to explain why. It's the same with the budget and variance numbers. ("Variance" just means difference.) If the actual number is way off budget—that is, if the variance is high—that's something else you'll need to look into (more about variance analysis in the toolbox at the end of this part). Hopefully your managers are on top of it. Financially savvy entrepreneurs and managers always identify variances to budget and find out why they occurred.

In the second case, the statement simply shows how the company is doing compared with last quarter or last year. Sometimes the point of comparison will be "same quarter last year." Again, if a number has moved in the wrong direction by a sizable amount, you will want to find out why.

In short, the point of these comparative income statements is to highlight what is changing, which numbers are where they are supposed to be, and which ones are not.

Footnotes

Chances are your company's income statement won't include footnotes. If it does, we recommend reading them very carefully. They are probably going to tell you something that the accountant thinks you should be aware of. Public companies' income statements, like those found in annual reports, are a little different. They usually include many, many footnotes. Some may be interesting, others not so much. But they provide the details behind the company's results. Depending on why you are reading the statement, those details may be of big interest to you.

Why so many? In cases where there is any question, the rules of accounting require the financial folks to explain how they arrived at their totals. So most of the notes are like windows into how the numbers were determined. Some are simple and straightforward, such as the following two footnotes from Nathan's Famous, Inc.'s 2007 Form 10-K (the annual report required by the Securities Exchange Act of 1934):

Fiscal Year—The Company's fiscal year ends on the last Sunday in March, which results in a 52- or 53-week reporting period. The results of operations and cash flows for the fiscal years ended March 25, 2007, March 26, 2006, and March 27, 2005 are all on the basis of 52-week reporting periods.

Interest Income—Interest income is recorded when it is earned and deemed realizable by the Company.[2]

But other footnotes can be long and complex, as suggested by the following footnote fragment from Build-A-Bear Workshop, Inc.'s Form 10-K for the fiscal year ending December 30, 2006:

Retail Revenue Recognition—Net retail sales are net of discounts, exclude sales tax, and are recognized at the time of sale. Shipping and handling costs billed to customers are included in net retail sales.

> *Revenues from the sale of gift cards are recognized at the time of re-*
> *demption. Unredeemed gift cards are included in gift cards and customer*
> *deposits on the consolidated balance sheets. The company escheats a portion*
> *of unredeemed gift cards according to Delaware escheatment regulations*
> *that require remittance of the cost of merchandise portion of unredeemed*
> *gift cards over five years old. The difference between the value of gift cards*
> *and the amount escheated is recorded as a reduction in selling, general,*
> *and administrative expenses in the consolidated statement of operations.*[3]

This particular footnote goes on for four more paragraphs. Don't get us wrong: it's important that Build-A-Bear Workshop explains its approach to revenue recognition. Decisions about when revenue is recognized are a key element of the art of finance. And don't assume that Nathan's Famous always has simple footnotes and Build-A-Bear Workshop always has complex ones. Our examples are simply to illustrate the diversity of the types of footnotes you'll find relating to the income statement in an annual report.

In reading your income statement, you'll want to be aware of some of the same material that public companies are required to put into their footnotes. Many you'll already know, such as the specifics of your fiscal year. Others you may know are being handled, but you might not know the details. As you increase your financial intelligence, we recommend asking lots of questions of your accountant about where the numbers came from and the assumptions used. You may get a surprised (or frustrated) look, but in the end this is *your* business. If you are going to make decisions based on the numbers, you better understand how they were arrived at.

ONE BIG RULE

So those are the rules for reading. But don't forget the one big rule that should be in the forefront of your thinking whenever you confront an income statement: *Many numbers on the statement reflect estimates and assumptions.* Accountants decide to include some transactions here and not there. They decide to estimate one way and not another. That is the art of finance. If you remember this one point, we assure you that your financial intelligence already exceeds that of many other entrepreneurs and business-people.

So let's plunge in for a more detailed look at some of the key categories. If you don't have another income statement handy, use the sample in appendix A for reference.

5

Revenue

The Issue Is Recognition

We'll begin at the top. We already noted that sales—the top line of an income statement—is also often called revenue. So far so good: only two words for the same thing isn't too bad, and we'll use both, just because they're so common. But watch out: some companies (and many people) call that top line income. In fact, the popular accounting software QuickBooks, a great product for new businesses, labels it income. That's *really* confusing because "income" more often means "profit," which is the *bottom* line. (Obviously, we have an uphill battle here. Where are the language police when you need them?)

A company can *record* or *recognize* a sale when it delivers a product or service to a customer. That's a simple principle. But as we suggested earlier, putting it into practice immediately runs into complexity. In fact, the issue of when a sale can be recorded is one of the more artful aspects of the income statement. Accountants have significant discretion over it, and entrepreneurs, therefore, must understand it thoroughly. So this is one place where your skills as an educated consumer of the financials will come in handy. If things don't seem right, ask questions—and if you can't get satisfactory answers, it might be time to be concerned. Your accountant or finance people might be making inappropriate or poorly thought-out decisions.

Sales

Sales or revenue is the dollar value of all the products or services a company provided to its customers during a given period of time.

MURKY GUIDELINES

The guideline that accountants use for recording or recognizing a sale is that the revenue must have been *earned.* A products company must have shipped the product. A service company must have performed the work. Fair enough—but what would you do about these situations?

- Your company does systems integration for corporate customers. A typical project requires six months to design and gain approval from the customer and then another twelve months to implement. The customer gets no real value from the project until the whole thing is complete. So when have you earned the revenue that the project generates?

- Your company sells to retailers. Using a practice known as bill-and-hold, you allow your customers to buy product (say, a popular Christmas item) well in advance of the time they will actually need it. You warehouse it for them and ship it out later. When have you earned the revenue?

- You own an architectural firm. The firm provides clients with plans for buildings, deals with the local building authorities, and supervises the construction or reconstruction. All these services are included in the firm's fee, which is generally figured as a percentage of construction costs. How do you figure out when the firm has earned its revenue?

We can't provide exact answers to these questions because accounting practices differ from one company to another. But that's precisely the point: there are no hard-and-fast answers. Project-based companies typically have rules that allow for partial revenue recognition when a project reaches certain milestones. Those rules, however, can vary. The "sales" figure on a company's top line always reflects the accountants' judgments about when they should recognize revenue. And where there is judgment, there is room for dispute—not to mention manipulation.

POSSIBILITIES FOR MANIPULATION

In fact, the pressures for manipulation can be intense. Say, for instance, that you started a software company. It sells software along with maintenance-and-upgrade contracts extending over a period of five years. So it always had to make a judgment about when to recognize revenue from a sale.

Now suppose your company did well and grew fast. Potential acquirers came shopping, and you sold the business to a large corporation, one that makes earnings predictions to Wall Street. The folks in the corporate office, like the folks in just about every publicly traded company, want to keep Wall Street happy. This quarter, alas, it looks as if the parent corporation is going to miss its earnings-per-share estimate by one penny. If it does, Wall Street will not be happy. And when Wall Street isn't happy, the company's stock gets hammered.

Aha! (You can hear the folks in the corporate office thinking.) Here is this new software division. Suppose we change how its revenue is recognized? Suppose we recognize 75 percent up front instead of 50 percent? The logic might be that a sale in this business takes a lot of initial work, so the accounting should reflect the cost and effort of making the sale as well as the cost of providing the product and delivering the service. Make the change—recognize the extra revenue—and suddenly earnings per share are nudged upward and now meet Wall Street's expectations.

Earnings per Share

In a publicly traded company, earnings per share (EPS) is a company's net profit divided by the number of shares outstanding. It's one of the numbers that Wall Street watches most closely. Wall Street has expectations for many companies' EPS, and if the expectations aren't met, the share price is likely to drop.

Interestingly, such a change is not illegal. An explanation might appear in a footnote to the financial statements, but then again it might not. Here is an example of a footnote explaining a change in how short-term investments are classified from IMAX Corporation's 2006 Form 10-K:

> *The Company has short-term investments which have maturities of more than three months and less than one year from the date of purchase. During November 2006, the Company changed the classification of these short-term investments from "held to maturity" to "available for sale" because the Company sold an investment (with a carrying value of $6.4 million) before its maturity date in order to meet its cash requirements at the time. The realized gain resulting from that sale was $0.02 million. As a consequence, the Company's short-term investments are accounted for at fair market value. Prior to November 2006, short-term investments were held at amortized cost and were classified as held to maturity based on the Company's positive intent and ability to hold the securities to maturity.*[1]

In principle, any accounting change that is material to the bottom line should be footnoted in this manner. But who decides what is material and what isn't? You guessed it: the accountants. In fact, it could very well be that recognizing 75 percent up front presents a more accurate picture of your software company's reality. But was the change in accounting method a result of good financial analysis, or did it reflect the need to make the earnings forecast? Could there be a bias lurking in there? Remember, accounting is the art of using limited data to come as close as possible to an accurate description of how well a company is performing. Revenue on the income statement is an estimate, a best guess. This example shows how estimates can introduce bias.

It isn't just business owners who have to be careful about bias; such decisions can directly affect your managers as well. Say you run a temporary staffing company with a couple of dozen full-time employees, many of them sales reps. Your sales manager focuses on the revenue numbers every month. She manages her people based on those numbers. She talks with them about their performance. Maybe she makes decisions about hiring and firing, and hands out rewards and recognition, all according to the numbers. Now you and your accountant decide to recognize revenue sooner, perhaps on the grounds that the new way better reflects reality. But did you tell the sales manager? If not, she's suddenly going to think her staff is doing great! Bonuses for everyone! But the underlying revenue figures might not look so good if they were recognized in the same way as before. If she didn't know the policy had changed and began passing out bonuses, she'd be paying for no real improvement. Financial intelligence in this case means understanding how the revenue is recognized, analyzing the real variances in the sales figures, and paying bonuses (or not) based on true changes in performance.

Just as an aside, the most common source of accounting fraud has been and probably always will be in that top line: sales. Sunbeam, Cendant, Xerox, and Rite Aid all played with revenue recognition in questionable ways. The issue is particularly acute in the software industry. Many software companies sell their products to resellers, who then sell the products to end users. Manufacturers, often under pressure from Wall Street to make their numbers, are frequently tempted to ship unordered software to these distributors at the end of a quarter. (The practice is known as channel stuffing.) One entrepreneurial company that took the high road in regard to this practice is Macromedia (now a part of Adobe), creators of the Internet Flash player and other products. When channel stuffing was becoming a serious problem in the industry, Macromedia voluntarily reported estimates of inventory held by its distributors, thereby showing that the channels for its products were not artificially loaded up. The message was clear to shareholders and employees alike: Macromedia was not going to be dragged into this practice.

The next time you read about a financial scandal in the paper, check first to see whether somebody was messing around with the revenue numbers. Unfortunately, it is all too common.

6

Costs and Expenses

No Hard-and-Fast Rules

Most entrepreneurs watch expenses closely. But did you know that there are plenty of estimates and biases on those expense lines? Let's examine the major line items.

COST OF GOODS SOLD OR COST OF SERVICES

As you probably do know, expenses on the income statement fall into two basic categories. The first is cost of goods sold, or COGS. As usual, there are a couple of different names for this category—in a service company, for instance, it may be called cost of services (COS). We've also frequently seen cost of revenue and cost of sales. (For simplicity's sake, we'll use the acronyms COGS or COS.) At any rate, what matters isn't the label; it's what's included. The idea behind COGS is to measure all the costs directly associated with making the product or delivering the service—the materials, the labor, and so on. If you suspect that rule is open to a ton of interpretation, you're on the money. Your bookkeeper or accountant has to make decisions about what to include in COGS and what to put somewhere else.

Some of these decisions are easy. In a manufacturing company, for instance, the following costs are definitely in:

- The wages of the people on the manufacturing line

- The cost of the materials that are used to make the product

  And plenty of costs are definitely out, such as:

- The cost of supplies (such as paper) used in the office

- The salary of the office manager

Ah, but then there's the gray area—and it's enormous. For example:

- What about the salary of the person who manages the plant where the product is manufactured?

- What about the wages of the plant supervisors?

- What about sales commissions?

Are all these directly related to the manufacturing of the product? Or are they operating expenses, like the cost of the office manager? We know of one company that includes direct selling costs in COGS. Its owners believe that doing so is appropriate for their business. There's the same ambiguity in a service environment. COS in a service company typically includes the labor associated with delivering the service. But what about the group supervisor? You could argue that his salary is part of general operations and therefore shouldn't be included in the COS line. You could also argue that he is supporting direct-service employees, so he should be included with them in that line. These are all judgment calls. There are no hard-and-fast rules.

The fact that there aren't any, frankly, is a little surprising. GAAP—the generally accepted accounting principles that govern how U.S. accountants keep their books—runs for some four thousand pages and spells out a lot of detailed rules. Public companies are required to follow GAAP. Privately owned companies aren't, but most do. If you use debt financing in your

Cost of Goods Sold (COGS) and Cost of Services (COS)

Cost of goods sold or cost of services is one category of expenses. It includes all the costs directly involved in producing a product or delivering a service.

> ## Operating Expenses (again)
>
> Operating expenses are the other major category of expenses. The category includes costs that are not directly related to making a product or delivering a service.

business, such as a line of credit based on accounts receivable, most banks and other financial institutions will require accounting procedures that adhere to GAAP.

You'd think GAAP would say, "The plant manager is out" or "The supervisor is in." No such luck; GAAP only provides guidelines. Companies take those guidelines and apply a logic that makes sense for their particular situations. The key, as accountants like to say, is reasonableness and consistency. So long as a company's logic is reasonable, and so long as that logic is applied consistently, whatever it wants to do is OK.

Why should a company owner care what's in and what's out? Consider the following scenarios:

• You own an architectural/engineering firm, and in the past your accountant has included salaries for the engineering analysts in COS. Now he suggests moving those costs out of COS, reasoning that the engineers really support the business as a whole. It's perfectly reasonable—even though engineering analysis has a lot to do with completing an architectural design, a case can be made that it isn't *directly* related to any particular job. So does the change matter? You

> ## GAAP
>
> GAAP stands for "generally accepted accounting principles." GAAP defines the standard for creating financial reports in the United States. It helps ensure the statements' validity and reliability, and it allows for easy comparison between companies and across industries. But GAAP doesn't spell out everything; it allows for plenty of discretion and judgment calls.

bet. Those salaries are no longer part of COS, or what's often called "above the line." As the business owner, you are going to look at your COS figure month in and month out, scrutinize it, wonder if it's at the right level. You may not scrutinize "below the line" expenses so carefully—after all, they include rent and a lot of other items that aren't easily changed. If you're not careful, engineering analysis will fall outside your radar.

- Your specialty manufacturing company is thriving, and your plant manager is charged with making a gross profit of $50,000 per month. One month he's $10,000 short. Then he realizes that $20,000 of his COGS is in a line item labeled "contract administration on plant orders." Does that really belong in COGS? Unbeknownst to you, he asks the accountants to move those costs to operating expenses. The accountants agree; the change is done. He hits his target and everyone is happy. You OK the move and promptly forget about it—after all, it's sort of a trivial matter. But then you might look at your trends and believe that gross margins are improving, all from a change in the way expenses were accounted for.

Again, these changes are legal, so long as they meet the reasonable-and-consistent test. You can even take an expense out of COGS one month and petition to put it back in next month. All you need is a reason good enough to convince the accountant (and in a public company, the auditor, if the changes are material to the company's financials). Of course, changing the rules constantly from one period to the next would be bad form. One thing we all need from our accountants is consistency.

Above the Line, Below the Line

The "line" generally refers to gross profit. Above that line on the income statement, typically, are sales and COGS or COS. Below the line are operating expenses, interest, and taxes. What's the difference? Items listed above the line tend to vary more (in the short term) than many of those below the line and so tend to get more managerial attention.

OPERATING EXPENSES: WHAT'S NECESSARY?

And where do costs go when they are taken out of COGS? Where is "below the line"? That's the other basic category of costs, namely operating expenses. Some companies refer to operating expenses as selling (or sales), general, and administrative expenses (SG&A, or just G&A), while others treat G&A as one subcategory and give sales and marketing its own line. Often a company will make this distinction based on the relative size of each. Rocky Mountain Chocolate Factory chooses to show sales and marketing on a separate line—sales and marketing are a significant portion of the company's expenses. By contrast, Ultralife Batteries includes sales and marketing with G&A, the more typical approach. Your company should follow the model of these companies: separate out whatever is most important so that you can track it easily.

Operating expenses are often thought of and referred to as overhead. The category includes items such as rent, utilities, telephone, research, and marketing. It also includes management and staff salaries—the office manager, accounting, IT, and so forth—plus everything else that the accountants have decided does not belong in COGS.

You can think of operating expenses as the cholesterol in a business. Good cholesterol makes you healthy, while bad cholesterol clogs your arteries. Good operating expenses make your business strong, and bad operating expenses drag down your bottom line and prevent you from taking advantage of business opportunities. (Another name for bad operating expenses is "unnecessary bureaucracy." Or "lard." You can probably come up with others. Even small companies are not immune.)

One more thing about COGS and operating expenses. You might think that COGS is the same as variable costs—costs that vary with the volume of production—and that operating expenses are fixed costs. Materials, for example, are a variable cost: the more you produce, the more material you have to buy. And materials are included in COGS. The salary of the office manager is a fixed cost, and that's included in operating expenses. Unfortunately, things aren't so simple here, either. For example, if supervisors' salaries are included in COGS, then that line item is fixed in the short run, whether you turn out one thousand widgets or fifty thousand. Or take selling expenses, which are typically part of SG&A. If you have a commissioned sales force, sales expenses are to some extent variable, but they are included in operating expenses, rather than COGS.

THE POWER OF DEPRECIATION AND AMORTIZATION

Another expense that is often buried in that SG&A line is depreciation and amortization. How this expense is treated can greatly affect the profit on an income statement.

We described an example of depreciation earlier in this part—buying a delivery truck and then spreading the cost over the three-year period that we assume the truck will be used for. As we said, that's an example of the matching principle. In general, depreciation is the expensing of a physical asset, such as a truck or a machine, over its estimated useful life. All this means is that the accountants figure out how long the asset is likely to be in use, take the appropriate fraction of its total cost for a given time period, and count that amount as an expense on the income statement for that time period.

In those few dry sentences, however, lurks a powerful tool that financial artists can put to work. It's worth going into some detail because you'll see exactly how assumptions about depreciation can affect any company's bottom line.

To keep things simple, let's assume we start a delivery company and line up a few customers. In the first full month of operation, we do $10,000 worth of business. At the start of that month, our company bought a $36,000 truck to make the deliveries. Since we're expecting the truck to last three years, we depreciate it at $1,000 a month (using the simple straight-line depreciation approach). So a greatly simplified income statement might look like this:

Revenue	$10,000
Cost of goods sold	5,000
Gross profit	5,000
Expenses	3,000
Depreciation	1,000
Net profit	$ 1,000

But our accountants don't have a crystal ball. They don't *know* that the truck will last exactly three years. They're making an assumption. Consider some alternative assumptions:

- They might assume the truck will last only one year, in which case they have to depreciate it at $3,000 a month. That takes $2,000 off the bottom line and moves the company from a net profit of $1,000 to a *loss* of $1,000.

- Or they could assume that it will last six years (seventy-two months). In that case, depreciation is only $500 a month, and net profit jumps to $1,500.

Hmm. In the former case, we're suddenly operating in the red. In the latter, we have increased net profit 50 percent—*just by changing one assumption about depreciation.* Accountants have to follow GAAP, of course, but GAAP allows plenty of flexibility. No matter what set of rules the accountants follow, estimating will be required whenever an asset lasts longer than a single accounting period. Your job is to understand those estimates and know how they affect the financials.

If you think this is purely an academic exercise, consider the sorry example of Waste Management Inc. (WMI), which we mentioned in the preface. WMI was one of the great corporate success stories of the 1970s and 1980s. So it came as a shock to everybody when the company announced in 1998 that it would take a pretax charge—a one-time write-off—of $3.54 *billion* against its earnings. Sometimes one-time charges are taken in advance of a restructuring, as we'll discuss later in this chapter. But this was different. In effect, WMI was admitting that it had been cooking its books on a previously unimaginable scale. It had actually earned $3.54 billion less in the previous several years than it had reported during that time.

What was going on? WMI had been a darling of Wall Street since the 1980s, when it began to grow rapidly by buying up other garbage companies. When the supply of garbage companies to buy began to dwindle, around 1992, it bought companies in other industries. But while it was pretty good at hauling trash, it didn't know how to run those other companies effectively. WMI's profit margins declined. Its share price plummeted.

Desperate to prop up the stock, executives began looking for ways to increase earnings.

Their gaze fell first on their fleet of twenty thousand garbage trucks, for which they had paid an average of $150,000 apiece. Up to that point, they had been depreciating the trucks over eight to ten years, which was the standard practice in the industry. That period wasn't long enough, the executives decided. A good truck could last twelve, thirteen, even fourteen years. When you add four years to your truck depreciation schedule, you can do wonderful things to your bottom line; it's like the preceding little example multiplied thousands of times over. But the executives didn't stop there. They realized that they had other assets they could do the same tricks with—about 1.5 million Dumpsters, for example. You could extend each Dumpster's depreciation period from the standard twelve years to, say, fifteen, eighteen, or twenty years, and you'd pick up another chunk of earnings per year. By fiddling with the depreciation numbers on the trucks and the Dumpsters, Waste Management's executives were able to pump up pretax earnings by a whopping $716 million. And this was just one of many tricks they used to make profits look larger than they were, which is why the end total was so huge.

Of course, the whole tangled web eventually came unraveled, as fraudulent schemes usually do. By then, however, it was too late to save the company. It was sold to a competitor, which kept the name but changed just about everything else. As for the perpetrators of the fraud, no criminal charges were ever filed against them, although some civil penalties were assessed.

Depreciation is a prime example of what accountants call a noncash expense. Right here, of course, is where they often lose the rest of us. How can an expense be other than cash? The key to that puzzling term is to remember that the cash has probably already been paid. The company already bought the truck. But the expense wasn't recorded that month, so it has to be recorded over the truck's life, a little at a time. No more money is going out the door; rather, it's just the accountants' way of figuring that *this* month's revenue depends on using that truck, so the income statement better have something in it that reflects the truck's cost. Incidentally, you should know that there are many methods to determine how to depreciate an asset. You don't need to know what they are; you can leave that to your

Noncash Expense

A noncash expense is one that is charged to a period on the income statement but is not actually paid out in cash. An example is depreciation: accountants deduct a certain amount each month for depreciation of equipment, but the company isn't obliged to pay out that amount, because the equipment was acquired in a previous period.

accountant. All you need to know is whether the use of the asset is matched appropriately to the revenue it is bringing in.

Amortization is the same basic idea as depreciation, but it applies to intangible assets. These days, intangible assets can be a big part of some companies' balance sheets. Items such as patents, copyrights, and goodwill (to be explained in chapter 9) are all assets—they cost money to acquire, and they have value—but they aren't physical assets like real estate and equipment. Still, they must be accounted for in a similar way. Take patents. If you run a biotech firm, you may have one or more patents in your portfolio. Your company had to buy those patents, or it had to do the R&D itself and then apply for the patent. Now the patents are helping bring in revenue, so the company must match the expense of the patents with the revenue the patents help generate, a little bit at a time. When an asset is intangible, though, accountants call that process amortization rather than depreciation. We're not sure why—but whatever the reason, it's a source of confusion.

Incidentally, economic depreciation implies that an asset loses its value over time. And indeed, a truck used in a delivery business does lose its value as it gets older. But accounting depreciation and amortization are more about cost allocation than about loss of value. A truck, for example, may be depreciated over three years so that its accounting value at the end of that time is zero, but it may still have some value on the open market. A patent may be amortized over its useful life, but if technology has advanced beyond it, the patent's value may be close to zero after a couple of years, regardless of what the accountants say. So assets are rarely worth what the books say they are worth. (We'll discuss accounting or "book" value in greater detail in part 3.)

ONE-TIME CHARGES: A YELLOW FLAG

Accounting is like life in at least one respect: there's a lot of stuff that doesn't fall neatly into categories. So every income statement—particularly in larger companies, but also in smaller ones—has a group of expenses that do not fall into COGS and are not operating expenses or overhead, either. Every statement is different, but typically you'll see lines for "other income/expense" (usually this is gain or loss from selling assets or from transactions unrelated to the operations of the business) and, of course, "taxes." As the business owner, you should know what is going into these numbers, but most of the time they are small and therefore don't have a big impact on profit. There is one line, however, that often turns up after COGS and operating expenses (though it is sometimes included under operating expenses)—a line that we think you should understand even though you may never run into this phenomenon in your own business. The most common label for this line is "one-time charge," and it is often critical to profitability. It's worth knowing about just in case you do come across it as you are studying other companies' financials.

You may occasionally have seen the phrase *taking the big bath* or something similar in the *Wall Street Journal*. That's a reference to these one-time charges, which are also known as *extraordinary items*, *write-offs*, *write-downs*, or *restructuring charges*. Sometimes write-offs occur, as in Waste Management's case, when a company has been doing something wrong and wants to correct its books. More often, one-time charges occur when a new CEO takes over a company and wants to restructure, reorganize, close plants, and maybe lay people off. It's the CEO's attempt, right or wrong, to improve the company based on his assessment of what the company needs. Normally, such a restructuring entails a lot of costs—paying off leases, offering severance packages, disposing of facilities, selling equipment, and so on. Anytime a business is forced to cut costs by laying off personnel, the costs associated with the layoff would likely fall into the one-time-charge area. Even small companies may want to delineate those charges in such a situation.

Now, accountants always want to be conservative. In fact, they're required to be. GAAP recommends that accountants record expenses as soon as they know that expenses will be incurred, even if they have to estimate exactly what the final figure will be. So when a restructuring occurs, accountants need to estimate those charges and record them.

Here is a big yellow flag—a truly terrific place for bias in the numbers to show up. After all, how do you really estimate the cost of restructuring? Accountants have a lot of discretion, and they're liable to be off the mark in one direction or another. If their estimate is too high—that is, if the actual costs are lower than expected—then part of that one-time charge has to be reversed. A reversed charge actually adds to profit in the new time period, so profits in that period wind up *higher* than they would otherwise have been—and all because an accounting estimate in a previous period was inaccurate! "Chainsaw Al" Dunlap, the notorious CEO of Sunbeam, was said to regard his accounting department as a profit center, and this fact may suggest why. (Incidentally, if you ever begin referring to your accountants in this manner, you and your company might have a problem.)

Of course, maybe the restructuring charge is too small. Then another charge has to be taken later. That clouds the numbers because the charge isn't really matched to any revenue in the new time period. This time around, profits are lower than they otherwise would be, again because the accountants made the wrong estimate in an earlier time frame. In the early 1990s, AT&T took "one-time" restructuring charges every year for several years. The company kept saying that earnings *before* the restructuring charges were growing—but it didn't make much difference, because after all those restructuring charges, the company was in pretty rough shape financially. Besides, if a company takes extraordinary one-time restructuring charges for several years in a row, how extraordinary can those charges really be?

Most of the shenanigans with restructuring occur in large, publicly traded companies. They're the ones, after all, that care about what Wall Street thinks. But if you ever intend to go public, or if you are looking at the income statement of a company you might acquire, you better understand one-time charges. They're an essential tool of accounting, but they easily lend themselves to financial obfuscation and mischief.

7

The Many Forms of Profit

So far we have covered sales or revenue—the top line—and costs and expenses. Revenue minus costs and expenses equals profit.

Of course, it might also equal *earnings*, *net income*, or even *net margin*. Amazingly enough, some companies use all these different terms for *profit*, sometimes in the same document. An income statement might have items labeled "gross margin," "operating income," "net profit," and (if it is a public company) "earnings per share." All these are the different types of profit typically seen on an income statement—and the company could just as easily have said "gross profit," "operating profit," "net profit," and "profit per share." When companies use different words right there in the same statement, it looks as if they are talking about different concepts. But they aren't.

So let's always use the term *profit* here and look at its various incarnations.

GROSS PROFIT: HOW MUCH IS ENOUGH?

Gross profit—revenue minus COGS or COS—is a key number for most companies. It tells you the basic profitability of your product or service. If that part of your business is not profitable, your company is probably not going to survive long. After all, how can you expect to pay below-the-line expenses, including your own salary, if you aren't generating a healthy gross profit?

Profit

Profit is the amount left over after expenses are subtracted from revenue. There are three basic types of profit: gross profit, operating profit, and net profit. Each one is determined by subtracting certain categories of expenses from revenue.

But what does *healthy* mean? How much gross profit is enough? That varies substantially by industry, and it's even likely to vary from one company to another in the same industry. In the grocery business, gross profit is typically a small percentage of sales. In the jewelry business, it's typically a much larger percentage. Other things being equal, a company with larger revenues can thrive with a lower gross profit percentage than a smaller one. (That's one reason why Wal-Mart can charge such low prices—it's so big.) To gauge your company's gross profit, you can compare it with industry standards, particularly for companies of a similar size. (Many industry trade groups offer benchmarks for various financial and nonfinancial measures.) You can also look at year-to-year trends, examining whether your gross profit is headed up or headed down. If it's headed down, you can ask why. Are production costs rising? Are you discounting too many sales? If gross profit is changing, understanding why helps you figure out where to focus your attention.

Here too, however, you need to keep a sharp eye out for possible bias in the numbers. *Gross profit can be greatly affected by decisions about when to recognize revenue and by decisions about what to include in COGS.* Suppose

Gross Profit

Gross profit is sales minus cost of goods sold or cost of services. It is what is left over after a company has paid the direct costs incurred in making the product or delivering the service. Gross profit must be sufficient to cover a business's operating expenses, taxes, financing costs, and net profit.

you run a market research firm, and you find that gross profit is headed downward. You look into the numbers, and at first it appears that service costs have gone up. So you begin thinking about cuts in service costs, perhaps even including some layoffs. But when you do more digging, you find that the accountants took some salaries that were previously in operating expenses and moved them into COGS. The change didn't seem material to them, so they never told you. Now you realize that service costs did not go up, and that laying off people would be a mistake. So you have to talk with the accountants. Why did they move those salaries? Why didn't they tell you? If those salaries are to remain in COGS, then maybe the firm's gross profit targets need to be reduced. But nothing else needs to change. You can see that by asking a few more questions, and by understanding the potential estimates and assumptions in the numbers, you can develop better information on which to base your decisions.

OPERATING PROFIT IS A KEY TO HEALTH

Operating profit—gross profit minus operating expenses or SG&A, including depreciation and amortization—is also known by the peculiar acronym EBIT (pronounced EE-bit). EBIT stands for earnings before interest and taxes. (Remember, *earnings* is just another name for profit). What has not yet been subtracted from revenue is interest and taxes. Why not? Because *operating profit is the profit a business earns from the business it is in*—from operations. Taxes don't really have anything to do with how well you are running your company. And interest expenses depend on whether the company is financed with debt or equity (we'll explain this difference in chapter 10). But the financial structure of the company doesn't say anything about how well it is run from an operational perspective.

So operating profit, or EBIT, is a good gauge of how well you and your management team are running your business. It measures both overall demand for the company's products or services (sales) and the company's efficiency in delivering those products or services (costs). Bankers and outside investors look at operating profit to see whether the company will be able to pay its debts and earn money for its shareholders. If you share your financials with others, vendors look at operating profit to see whether the company will be able to pay its bills. (As we'll see later, however, operating

Operating Profit, or EBIT

Operating profit is gross profit minus operating expenses, which include depreciation and amortization. In other words, it shows the profit made from running the business.

profit is not always the best gauge of this.) And if customers have an opportunity to see your financials, the larger ones examine operating profit to ascertain whether your company is doing an efficient job and is likely to be around for a while. Even savvy managers may check out the operating profit figures if they get a chance to see the financials. A healthy and growing operating profit suggests that managers and employees are going to be able to keep their jobs and may have opportunities for advancement.

However, remember that potential biases in the numbers can impact operating profit as well. Are there any one-time charges? What is the depreciation line? As we have seen, depreciation can be altered to affect profit one way or another. For a while, Wall Street analysts were watching public companies' operating profit, or EBIT, closely. But some of the companies that were later revealed to have committed fraud turned out to be playing games with depreciation (remember Waste Management), so their EBIT numbers were suspect. Before long, Wall Street began focusing on another number—EBITDA (pronounced EE-bit-dah), or earnings before interest, taxes, depreciation, and amortization. Some people think EBITDA is a better measure of a company's operating efficiency because it ignores noncash charges such as depreciation altogether.

NET PROFIT AND HOW TO FIX IT

Now, finally, let's get to the bottom line: net profit. It is usually the last line on the income statement. *Net profit* is what is left over after everything is subtracted—cost of goods sold or cost of services, operating expenses, taxes, interest, one-time charges, and noncash expenses such as depreciation and amortization. When someone asks, "What's the bottom line?" in reference to a company's financial performance, he or she is almost always referring to net profit. Some of the key numbers used to measure a public company, such as earnings per share and the price-earnings (P/E) ratio, are based on net profit. Yet, it is strange that financial folks don't call it profit per share and the price-profit ratio. But they don't.

What if your company's net profit is lower than it ought to be? Aside from monkeying with the books, there are only three possible fixes for low profitability. One, you can increase profitable sales. This solution almost always requires a good deal of time. You have to find new markets or new prospects, work through the sales cycle, and so on. Two, you can figure out how to lower production costs and run more efficiently—that is, reduce COGS. This, too, takes time: you need to study the production process, find the inefficiencies, and implement changes. Three, you can cut operating expenses, which almost always means reducing the headcount in your company. This is usually the only short-term solution available. That's why we hear that so many CEOs who take over a troubled public company start by cutting the payroll in the overhead expense areas. It makes profits look better fast.

Of course, layoffs can backfire. Morale suffers. Good people whom the new CEO wants to keep may begin looking for jobs elsewhere. And that's not the only danger. For example, "Chainsaw Al" Dunlap used the lay-people-off strategy a number of times to pump up the profit of companies he took over, and Wall Street usually rewarded him for it. But the strategy didn't work when he got to Sunbeam. Yes, he slashed headcount, and yes, profit rose. In fact, Wall Street was so enthusiastic about the company's pumped-up profitability that it bid Sunbeam's shares way up. But Dunlap's strategy all along had been to sell the company at a profit—and now, with its shares selling at a premium, the company was too expensive for pro-

Net Profit

Net profit is the bottom line of the income statement: what's left after all costs and expenses are subtracted from revenue. It's operating profit minus interest expenses, taxes, one-time charges, and any other costs not included in operating profit.

spective buyers to consider. Without a buyer, Sunbeam was forced to limp along until its problems became apparent and Dunlap was forced out by the board.

The moral? For most companies, and we bet yours is included, it's better to manage for the long haul and to focus on increasing profitable sales and reducing costs. Sure, operating expenses may have to be trimmed. But if that's your only focus, you're probably just postponing the day of reckoning.

If you would like to try your hand at reading and analyzing an income statement to practice what you have learned—or if you just need a break from reading and want to do something—please turn to the income statement exercise in appendix B.

Part Two
TOOLBOX

UNDERSTANDING VARIANCE

Variance just means difference. It might be the difference between budget and actual for the month or year, between actual this month and actual last month, and so on. It can be presented in dollars or percentages, or both. Percentages are usually more useful because they provide a quick and easy basis of comparison between the two numbers.

The only difficulty with variance comes with determining whether a variance is favorable or unfavorable. More revenue than expected, for instance, is favorable, but more expense than expected is unfavorable. Sometimes your accountant or financial staff are helpful and let you know in a note that a variance enclosed in parentheses or a variance preceded by a minus sign is unfavorable. But often you have to figure it out on your own. We recommend doing a few calculations yourself, determining whether the indicated variances are bad or good and then checking to see how they are displayed. Be sure to do the calculations for both a revenue line item and an expense line item. Sometimes parentheses or negative signs indicate only the mathematical difference between two numbers. In that case, parentheses for a revenue line item might mean favorable, and parentheses for an expense line item might mean unfavorable.

CALCULATING PERCENT OF AND PERCENT CHANGE

When you're studying the income statement, there are two simple yet powerful tools that can help you understand the meaning behind the numbers.

The first is "percent of" calculations. *Percent of* determines what percentage something is of something else. The basic formula is:

$$\text{percent of} = \frac{\text{part}}{\text{whole}}$$

For example, if you had $75 in your wallet and gave a friend $6, you've given him 8 percent of what you had.

$$\frac{\$6}{\$75} = .08$$

(Remember that to convert a decimal to a percentage, you move the decimal point over two places to the right, so that .08 becomes 8 percent.)

So, for example, if you wanted to analyze your budget from last year, you might wonder how much of your budget was spent on supplies. Assume that your company spent $6,000 on supplies last year and that its total office budget was $50,000. So the calculation is as follows:

$$\frac{\$6,000}{\$50,000} = .12 = 12\%$$

The second tool is percent change. (The percent change formula is also the formula for percent variance—so once you have percent change down, you can also do percent variance.) Percent change is simply the percentage something changed from one period to the next, from budget to actual, from forecast to actual, and so on (you get the idea).

The formula for percent change from one year to the next is as follows:

$$\frac{\text{current year} - \text{prior year}}{\text{prior year}}$$

For example, if prior year revenue was $3,000 and current year revenue was $3,750, then the percent change is as follows:

$$\frac{\$3,750 - \$3,000}{\$3,000} = .25 = 25\%$$

In general, the formula for percent change is as follows:

$$\frac{\text{final value} - \text{initial value}}{\text{initial value}}$$

You will find more opportunities to practice these percent of and percent change calculations in the practice exercises in appendix B.

The Balance Sheet Reveals the Most

8

Understanding
Balance Sheet Basics

There's a puzzling fact about financial statements. Maybe you've noticed it.

Give a company's financials to a first-time entrepreneur, and the first thing he will turn to is the income statement. Entrepreneurs know that a company has to make a profit. Maybe he has worked in other companies and has had P&L responsibility. Or maybe this is his first business experience, and he knows revenue has to exceed expenses. He believes that the income statement is the best record of a company's financial performance. So that's what he looks at first.

Now try giving the same set of financials to a banker, an experienced investor, or maybe a veteran entrepreneur. The first statement this person will turn to is invariably the balance sheet. In fact, she's likely to pore over it for some time. Then she'll start flipping the pages, checking out the income statement and the cash flow statement—but always going back to the balance sheet.

Why don't less-experienced entrepreneurs do what the pros do? Why do they limit their attention to the income statement? We chalk it up to three factors:

- The balance sheet is a little harder to get your mind around than the income statement. The income statement, after all, is pretty intuitive. The balance sheet isn't—at least, not until you understand the basics.

- Company owners deal with revenue and expenses day in and day out. They monitor sales. They create and approve expense budgets, and usually the budget categories more or less align with the line items on the income statement. Balance sheet data, by contrast, rarely figures in the day-to-day management of a young company (although you'll see why we think it should).

- Managing the balance sheet requires a deeper understanding of finance than managing an income statement. You not only have to know what the various categories refer to; you have to know how they fit together. You also have to understand how changes in the balance sheet affect the other financial statements, and vice versa.

Maybe you, too, are a bit wary of the balance sheet. But remember, what we're focusing on here is financial intelligence—understanding how financial results are measured and what you as a company owner can do to make your business more successful. We won't get into the esoteric elements of the balance sheet, just the ones you need to appreciate the art of this statement and do the analyses of your business that the statement makes possible.

SHOWING WHERE THINGS STAND RIGHT NOW

So what is the balance sheet? *It's no more, and no less, than a statement of what a business owns and what it owes at a particular point in time.* The difference between what a company owns and what it owes represents *equity*. Just as one of a company's goals is to increase profitability, another is to increase equity. And as it happens, the two are intimately related.

What is this relationship? Consider an analogy. Profitability is sort of like the grade you receive for a course in college. You spend a semester writing papers and taking exams. At the end of the semester, the instructor tallies your performance and gives you an A– or a C+ or whatever. Equity is more like your overall grade point average (GPA). Your GPA always reflects your cumulative performance, but at only one point in time. Any one grade affects it but doesn't determine it. The income statement affects the balance sheet much the way an individual grade affects your GPA. Make a

Equity

Equity is the shareholders' stake in the company as measured by accounting rules. It's also called the company's book value. In accounting terms, equity is always assets minus liabilities; it is also the sum of all capital paid in by shareholders plus any profits earned by the company since its inception minus dividends paid out to shareholders. That's the accounting formula, anyway; remember that what a company's shares are actually worth is whatever a willing buyer will pay for them.

profit in any given period, other things being equal, and the equity on your balance sheet will show an increase. Lose money, and it will show a decrease. Over time, the equity section of the balance sheet shows the *accumulation* of profits or losses left in the business; the line is called retained earnings (losses) or sometimes accumulated earnings (deficit).

Here too, however, understanding the balance sheet means understanding all the assumptions, decisions, and estimates that go into it. Like the income statement, the balance sheet is in many respects a work of art, not just a work of calculation.

INDIVIDUALS AND BUSINESSES

Since the balance sheet is so important, we want to begin with some simple lessons. Bear with us—it's important in this case to crawl before you walk. Besides, if you want to explain your company's balance sheet to your employees or family members, you'll probably want to begin at the beginning.

So here's a way to go about it. Start by considering an individual's financial situation, or financial worth, at a given point in time. You add up what the person owns, subtract what she owes, and come up with her net worth:

owns − owes = net worth

Another way to state the same thing is this:

$$\text{owns} = \text{owes} + \text{net worth}$$

For an individual, the ownership category might include cash in the bank, big-ticket items like a house and a car, and all the other property the person can lay claim to. It also would include financial assets such as stocks and bonds or a 401(k) account. The "owing" category includes outstanding mortgage, car loan, and credit card balances, as well as any other debt. Note that we're avoiding for the moment the question of how to calculate some of those numbers. What's the value of the house—what the person paid for it or what it might bring today? How about the car or the TV? You can see the art of finance peeking around the curtain here—but more on that in a moment.

Now move from an individual to a business. Same concepts, different language:

• What the company owns is called its *assets*.

• What it owes is called its *liabilities*.

• What it's worth is called *owners' equity* or *shareholders' equity*.

And the basic equation now looks like this:

$$\text{assets} - \text{liabilities} = \text{owners' equity}$$

or this:

$$\text{assets} = \text{liabilities} + \text{owners' equity}$$

If you took any sort of accounting course in school, you learned one of these formulas. The instructor probably called it the fundamental accounting equation. You also learned that the latter formulation reflects the two sides of the balance sheet: assets on the one side, liabilities and owners' equity on the other. The sum on one side has to equal the sum on the other side; the balance sheet has to balance. Before you finish this part of the book, you will understand why.

READING A BALANCE SHEET

First, however, find a sample balance sheet, either your own company's or one in an annual report. (Or just look at the sample in appendix A.) Since

Fiscal Year

A fiscal year is any twelve-month period that a company uses for accounting purposes. Many companies use the calendar year, but some use other periods (October 1 to September 30, for example). Some retailers use a specific weekend, such as the last Sunday of the year, to mark the end of their fiscal year. You must know a company's fiscal year to ascertain how recent the information you are looking at is.

the balance sheet shows a company's financial situation at a given point in time, there should be a specific date at the top. It's usually the end of a month, quarter, year, or fiscal year. When you're looking at financial statements together, you typically want to see an income statement for a month, quarter, or year, along with the balance sheet for the end of the period reported. (Unlike income statements, balance sheets are almost always for an entire organization. Sometimes a large corporation creates subsidiary balance sheets for its operating divisions, but it rarely does so for a single facility.) As we'll see, accounting professionals have to do some estimating on the balance sheet, just the way they do with the income statement. Remember our hypothetical delivery business? The way we depreciate the truck affects not only the income statement but also the value of assets shown on the balance sheet. It turns out that the assumptions and biases in the income statement flow into the balance sheet one way or another.

Balance sheets come in two typical formats. The traditional model shows assets on the left-hand side of the page and liabilities and owners' equity on the right side, with liabilities at the top. The less traditional format puts assets on top, liabilities in the middle, and owners' equity on the bottom. Whatever the format, the balance remains the same: assets must equal liabilities plus owners' equity. (In the nonprofit world, owners' equity is sometimes called net assets.) Often a balance sheet shows comparative figures for, say, December 31 of the most recent year and December 31 of the previous year. Check the column headings to see what points in time are being compared.

As with income statements, some organizations (usually public companies) have unusual line items on their balance sheets that you won't find discussed in this book. Remember, many of these items may be clarified in the footnotes. For public companies, the footnotes will appear in the 10-K right after the financial statements; in fact, the balance sheets of large public companies are notorious for their footnotes. Ford Motor Company's 2006 annual report contained a whopping fifty-one pages of notes, many of them pertaining to the balance sheet. Indeed, companies often include a standard disclaimer in the notes that makes the very point about the art of finance that we are making in this book. Big Dog Holdings, Inc., for instance, says this in its 2006 report:

Use of Estimate

The preparation of financial statements in conformity with accounting principles generally accepted in the United States of America requires management to make estimates and assumptions that affect the reported amounts of assets and liabilities and disclosure of contingent assets and liabilities at the date of the financial statements and the reported amounts of revenues and expenses during the reporting period. Actual results could differ from those estimates.[1]

If your accountant includes notes with your balance sheet and you are unclear about what they mean, be sure to ask him. This is your business, and you should be aware of the assumptions and calculations that go into your numbers.

Since the balance sheet is new to many entrepreneurs, we want to walk you through the most common line items. Some may look strange at first, but don't worry: just keep in mind that distinction between "owned" and "owed." As with the income statement, we'll pause along the way to see which lines are most easily monkeyed with.

9

Assets

More Estimates and Assumptions
(Except for Cash)

Assets are what the company owns: cash and securities, machinery and equipment, buildings and land, whatever. *Current assets*, which usually come first on the balance sheet, include anything that can be turned into cash in less than a year. *Long-term assets* are those that have a useful life of more than a year.

TYPES OF ASSETS

Within those broad categories, of course, are many line items. We'll list the most common ones—those that appear on nearly every company's balance sheet.

Cash and Cash Equivalents

Cash and cash equivalents are the hard stuff. Money in the bank. Money in money-market accounts. Also publicly traded stocks and bonds that are owned by the company—the kind you can turn into cash in a day or less if you need to. Another name for this category is *liquid assets*. This is one of the few line items that are not subject to accountants' discretion. When Microsoft says it has $56 billion in cash and short-term investments, or whatever the latest number is, it means it really has that much in banks, money funds, and publicly traded securities. Of course, companies can lie. The giant Italian company Parmalat reported on its balance sheet that it had billions in an account with Bank of America. It didn't.

Accounts Receivable

Accounts receivable, or A/R, is the amount customers owe the company. Remember, revenue is a promise to pay, so accounts receivable includes all the promises that haven't yet been collected. Why is this an asset? Because all or most of these commitments will convert to cash that soon *will* belong to the company. An account receivable is like a loan from the company to its customers—and the company owns the customers' obligation. Accounts receivable is one line item that business owners need to watch closely, since it has a lot to do with the cash that will, or will not, come in. Creditors are likely to be watching it as well. We'll say more on how to manage accounts receivable in part 7, on working capital.

Sometimes a balance sheet includes an item labeled "allowance for bad debt" that is subtracted from accounts receivable. This is the accountant's estimate—usually based on past experience—of the dollars owed by customers who don't pay their bills. In many companies, subtracting a bad-debt allowance provides a more accurate reflection of the value of those accounts receivable. But note well: estimates are already creeping in. In fact, many public companies use the bad-debt reserve as a tool to "smooth" their profit (remember, Wall Street is watching them). When they *increase* the bad-debt reserve on the balance sheet, they have to record an expense

"Smoothing" Earnings

You might think that Wall Street would like a big spike in a public company's profits—more money for shareholders, right? But if the spike is unforeseen and unexplained—and especially if it catches Wall Street by surprise—investors are likely to react negatively, taking it as a sign that management isn't in control of the business. So companies like to "smooth" their earnings—that is, their profit—thus maintaining steady and predictable growth.

against profit on the income statement. That lowers their reported profit. When they *decrease* the bad debt reserve, similarly, the adjustment increases profit on the income statement. Since the bad-debt reserve is always an estimate, there is room here for subjectivity.

Inventory

Service companies typically don't have much in the way of inventory, but nearly every other company—manufacturers, wholesalers, retailers—does. One part of the inventory figure is the value of the products that are ready to be sold. That's called *finished-goods inventory.* A second part, usually relevant only to manufacturers, is the value of products that are under construction. Accountants dub that *work-in-process inventory*, or just WIP (pronounced "whip"). Then, of course, there's the inventory of raw materials that will be used to make products. That's called—stand back—*raw-materials inventory.*

Accountants can (and do!) spend days on end talking about ways of valuing inventory. We plan to spend no time at all on the subject. However, you should know that different methods of inventory valuation can often alter the assets side of a balance sheet significantly. If a company changes its method of valuing inventory during a given year, that fact should appear in a footnote to its balance sheet. Many companies detail how they accounted for their inventories in the footnotes, as Crocs, Inc. did in its 2007 Form 10-K:

Inventories

Raw materials and supplies are valued at the lower of cost, replacement cost, or net realizable value. Work in process and finished goods are valued at the lower of cost and net realizable value. Cost is determined on the first in, first out basis. The cost of work in process and finished goods consists of the cost of raw materials and an applicable share of the cost of labor and manufacturing overhead.[1]

If you have questions about how your accountants are valuing your inventory, be sure to ask them. What you do need to remember as a business owner, however, is that all inventory costs money. It is created at the expense of cash. (Maybe you've heard the expression "All our cash is tied up in inventory," though we hope it doesn't apply to you.) In fact, this is one way companies can improve their cash position. Decrease your inventory, other things being equal, and you raise your company's cash level. And if your company's financial resources are tight (as they are for many entrepreneurial companies), watching and managing inventory is going to be important. A company always wants to carry as little inventory as possible, provided that it still has materials ready for its manufacturing processes and products ready when customers come calling. We'll come back to this topic later in the book.

Property, Plant, and Equipment

Another line on the balance sheet—property, plant, and equipment (PPE)—includes buildings, machinery, trucks, computers, and every other physical asset a company owns. The PPE figure is the total number of dollars it cost to buy all the facilities and equipment the company uses to operate the business. Note that the relevant cost here is the *purchase price.* Without constant appraisals, nobody really knows how much a company's real estate or equipment might be worth on the open market. So accountants, governed by the principle of conservatism, say in effect, "Let's use what we do know, which is the cost of acquiring those assets."

Another reason for using the purchase price is to avoid more opportunities to bias the numbers. Suppose an asset—land, for example—has actually increased in value. If we wanted to mark it up on the balance sheet to its current value, we would have to record a profit on the income statement. But that profit would be based simply on someone's opinion about what the land is worth today. This is not a good idea. Some companies— think Enron—go so far as to set up corporate shells, often owned by a company executive or other insider, and then sell assets to those shells. That allows them to record a profit, just the way they would if they were selling off assets. But it is not the kind of profit investors or lenders like to see.

The fact that companies must rely on purchase price to value their assets, of course, can create some striking anomalies. Say you started an entertainment company thirty years ago, and you bought land around Los Angeles for $500,000. The land could be worth $5 million today—but it will still be valued at $500,000 on the balance sheet. Sophisticated investors like to nose around in public companies' balance sheets in hopes of finding such undervalued assets.

Less: Accumulated Depreciation

Land doesn't wear out, so accountants don't record any depreciation each year. But buildings and equipment do. The point of accounting depreciation, however, isn't to estimate what the buildings and equipment are worth right now; the point is to allocate the investment in the asset over the time it is used to generate revenue and profits (remember the matching principle in chapter 3). The depreciation charge is a way of ensuring that the income statement accurately reflects the true cost of producing goods or delivering services. To calculate *accumulated* depreciation, accountants simply add up all the charges for depreciation they have taken since the day an asset was bought.

We showed you in a previous chapter how a company can magically go from unprofitable to profitable just by changing the way it depreciates its assets. That art-of-finance magic extends to the balance sheet as well. If a company decides its trucks can last six years rather than three, it will record a 50 percent smaller charge on its income statement year after year. That means less accumulated depreciation on the balance sheet, a higher figure for net PPE, and thus more assets. More assets, by the fundamental accounting equation, translate into more owners' equity.

Goodwill

Goodwill is found on the balance sheets of companies that have acquired other companies. It's the difference between the price paid for the acquired

Acquisitions

An acquisition occurs when one company buys another. Often you'll see in the newspaper the words *merger* or *consolidation*. Don't be fooled: one company still bought the other. A more neutral-sounding term may make the deal seem more palatable to the owners, employees, or customers of the acquired company, but it is still an acquisition.

company and the net assets the acquirer actually got. (Net assets, again, refer to the fair market value of the acquiree's assets minus the liabilities assumed by the acquirer.)

The idea isn't as complex as it sounds. Say you're the CEO of a successful company that is on the acquisition trail. You spot a nice little warehousing business called MJQ Storage that fits your needs perfectly. You agree to buy MJQ for $5 million. By the rules of accounting, if you pay in cash, the asset labeled cash on your balance sheet will decrease by $5 million. That means other assets have to rise by $5 million. After all, the balance sheet still has to balance. And you haven't done anything so far that would change liabilities or owners' equity.

Now watch closely. Since you are buying a collection of physical assets (among other things), you will appraise those assets the way any buyer would. Maybe you decide that MJQ's buildings, shelving, forklifts, and computers are worth $2 million, after deducting whatever liabilities you are assuming. That doesn't mean you made a bad deal. You are buying a going concern with a name, a customer list, talented and knowledgeable employees, and so on, and these so-called intangibles can in some cases be much more valuable than the tangible assets. (How much would you pay for the brand name Coca-Cola? Or for Dell's customer list?) In our example, you're buying $3 million worth of intangibles. Accountants call that $3 million goodwill. The $3 million of goodwill and the $2 million of net physical assets add up to the $5 million you paid and the corresponding $5 million increase in assets on the balance sheet.

And now we want to tell a little story about goodwill that shows the art of finance at work.

In years past, goodwill was amortized. (Remember, amortization is the same idea as depreciation, except that it applies to intangible assets.) Other assets were typically depreciated over two to five years, but goodwill could be amortized over a maximum of forty years, or the estimated useful life of the acquired business.

Then the rule changed. The people who write those generally accepted accounting principles—the Financial Accounting Standards Board, or FASB (pronounced faz-bee)—decided that if goodwill consists of the reputation, the customer base, and so on of the company you are buying, then all those assets don't lose value over time. They actually may become more valuable over time. In short, goodwill is more like land than it is like equipment. So not amortizing it helps accountants portray that accurate reflection of reality that they are always seeking.

But look at the effect. When you bought MJQ Storage, you wound up with $3 million worth of goodwill on your balance sheet, and let's say you estimated the useful life of that goodwill at thirty years. Before the rule change, you would have amortized the goodwill over thirty years at $100,000 per year. In other words, you would have deducted $100,000 a year from revenues, thereby reducing the profitability of your company by the same amount. Meanwhile, you're depreciating MJQ's physical assets over, say, a four-year period at $500,000 per year. Again, that $500,000 would be subtracted from revenue to determine profit.

So what happens? Before the rule change, other things being equal, you wanted to have *more* goodwill and *less* in physical assets, simply because goodwill is amortized over a longer period of time, so the amount subtracted from revenue to determine profit is less (which keeps profits higher). You had an incentive to shop for companies where most of what you'd be buying was goodwill, and you had an incentive to *undervalue* the physical assets of the company you were buying. (Remember, it is your own people who are doing the appraisal of those assets!)

With the new rule, goodwill sits on the books and isn't amortized. Nothing at all is subtracted from revenue, and profitability is correspondingly higher. You now have even more of an incentive to look for companies without much in the way of physical assets, and even more of an incentive to undervalue those assets. Tyco was one company that was accused of taking

Intangibles

A company's intangible assets include anything that has value but that you can't touch or spend: employees, proprietary knowledge, patents, brand names, reputation, strategic strengths, and so on. Most of these assets are not found on the balance sheet unless an acquiring company pays for them and records them as goodwill. The exception is intellectual property, such as patents and copyrights, which can be shown on the balance sheet and amortized over its useful life.

advantage of this rule. In the go-go years of 2000 and 2001, Tyco was buying companies at breakneck speed—more than six hundred in those two years alone. Many analysts thought that Tyco regularly undervalued the assets of these numerous companies. Doing so would increase the goodwill included in all those acquisitions and lower the depreciation Tyco had to take each year. That, in turn, would make profit higher and would drive up Tyco's share price.

But eventually, analysts and investors noticed that Tyco had so much goodwill on its books and so little (relatively speaking) in the way of physical assets, that if you took goodwill out of the balance sheet equation, the company's liabilities were actually higher than its assets. This is not a situation investors like to see.

Intellectual Property, Patents, and Other Intangibles

How do you account for the cost of creating a new software program that you expect to generate revenue for years? What about the cost of developing a new wonder drug, which is protected by a twenty-year patent (from the date of application)? Obviously, it makes no sense to record the whole cost as an expense on the income statement in any given period, any more than you would record the whole cost of buying a truck. Like a truck, the software and the patent will help generate revenue in future accounting periods. So these investments are considered intangible assets and should be amortized over the life of the revenue stream they generate. By the same token, however, R&D expenses that do not result in an asset likely to generate revenue should be recorded as an expense on the income statement.

You can see the potential for subjectivity here. GAAP says that R&D can be amortized if the product under development is technologically feasible. But who determines technological feasibility? Again, we are back in the realm of art. If a company decides that its R&D projects are technologically feasible, it can amortize those sums over time and make its profits look higher. Otherwise, it must expense R&D costs as they are incurred—a more conservative approach. Computer Associates is one company that got itself into trouble for amortizing R&D on products that had a questionable future. Like depreciation, amortization decisions can often have a sizable effect on profitability and owners' equity.

Accruals and Prepaid Assets

To explain accruals and prepaid assets, let's look at a hypothetical example. Say you start a high-end bicycle manufacturing company, and you rent manufacturing space for the entire year for $60,000. Since your company is a lousy credit risk—nobody likes to do business with a start-up for just this reason—the landlord insists on payment up front.

Now, we know from the matching principle that it doesn't make sense to book the entire $60,000 in January as an expense on the income statement. It's rent for the whole year. It has to be spread out over the year, so that the cost of the rent is matched to the revenue that it helped bring in. So in January you put $5,000 on the income statement for rent. But where does the other $55,000 go? You have to keep track of it somewhere. Well, prepaid rent is one example of a prepaid asset. You have bought something—you own the rights to that space for a year—so it is an asset. And you keep track of assets on the balance sheet.

Every month, of course, you'll have to move $5,000 out of the prepaid-asset line on the balance sheet and put it in the income statement as an expense for rent. That's called an accrual, and the account on the balance sheet that records what has not yet been expensed is called an *accrued asset account.* Though the terms are confusing, note that the practice is still conservative: we're keeping track of all our known expenses, and we're also tracking what we paid for in advance.

But the art of finance can creep in here as well because there is room for judgment on what to accrue and what to charge in any given period. Say, for example, your company is developing a major advertising campaign. The work is all done in January, and it comes to $100,000. The accountants might decide that this campaign will benefit the company for two years, so they would book the $100,000 as a prepaid asset and charge one-twenty-fourth of the cost each month on the income statement. A company facing a tough month is likely to decide that this is the best course—after all, it's better to deduct one-twenty-fourth of $100,000 from profits than the whole amount. But what if January is a great month? Then the company might decide to expense the entire campaign—charge it all against January's revenue—because, well, the accountants can't be sure that it will help generate revenue during the next two years. Now the company has an advertising campaign that's all paid for, and profits in the months to come will be correspondingly higher. In a perfect world, our accounting friends would have a crystal ball to tell them exactly how long that advertising campaign will generate revenue. Since they don't yet have such a device, they must rely on estimates.

So that's it for assets. Add them all up, along with whatever extraneous items you might find, and you get the "total assets" line at the bottom of the left side of the balance sheet. Now it's time to move on to the other side—liabilities and owners' equity.

10

On the Other Side

Liabilities and Equity

We said earlier that liabilities are what a company owes and that equity is its net worth. There's another—only slightly different—way to look at this side of the balance sheet, which is that *it shows how the assets were obtained.* If a company borrows funds in any way, shape, or form to obtain an asset, the borrowing is going to show up on one or another of the liabilities lines. If its owners put money into the business (and of course, receive stock) to obtain an asset, that will be reflected on one of the lines under owners' equity. This way of looking at this side of the balance sheet can be important to an entrepreneur. It gives you a picture of how your company is funded, which is critical to any future decisions about debt and equity. Funding a business with debt is usually more risky because of the legal responsibility to pay back the debt. Equity, on the other hand, requires giving up partial ownership in the business, if you are selling shares to anyone besides yourself.

TYPES OF LIABILITIES

But first things first, which on this side of the balance sheet means liabilities, the financial obligations a company owes to other entities. Liabilities are always divided into two main categories. *Current liabilities* are those that have to be paid off in less than a year. *Long-term liabilities* are those that come due over a longer time frame. Liabilities are usually listed on the balance sheet from shortest term to longest term, so the very layout tells you something about what's due when.

Current Portion of Long-Term Debt

If your company owes $100,000 to a bank on a long-term loan, maybe $10,000 of it is due this year. So that's the amount that shows up in the current-liabilities section of the balance sheet. The line will be labeled "current portion of long-term debt" or something like that. The other $90,000 shows up under "long-term liabilities."

Short-Term Loans

Short-term loans are lines of credit and short-term revolving loans. These credit lines are usually secured by current assets, such as accounts receivable and inventory. The entire balance outstanding is shown here.

Accounts Payable

Accounts payable shows the amount the company owes its vendors. The company receives goods and services from suppliers every day and typically doesn't pay the bill for at least thirty days. The vendors, in effect, have loaned the company money. Accounts payable shows how much was owed on the date of the balance sheet. Any balance on a company's credit cards is usually included in accounts payable.

Accrued Expenses and Other Short-Term Liabilities

The catchall category of accrued expenses and other short-term liabilities includes everything else the company owes. One example is payroll. Let's assume that your office manager gets paid on October 1. Does it make sense to charge her pay as an expense on the income statement in October? Probably not—her October paycheck is for work performed in September. So the accountants would figure out or estimate how much the company owes her on October 1 for work completed in September and then charge those expenses to September. This is an accrued liability. It's like an internal bill in September for a payment to be made in October. Accrued liabilities are part of the matching principle—we have matched expenses with the revenue they help bring in every month.

Long-Term Liabilities

Most long-term liabilities are loans. But there are also other liabilities that you might see listed here. Examples include deferred bonuses or compensation and deferred taxes. If these other liabilities are substantial, this section of the balance sheet needs to be watched closely.

OWNERS' EQUITY

Finally—owners' equity! Remember the equation? Owners' equity is what's left after we subtract liabilities from assets. Equity includes the capital provided by you and the other investors in your company and the profits retained by the company over time. Owners' equity goes by many names, including shareholders' equity and stockholders' equity. The owners' equity line items listed in some companies' balance sheets can be quite detailed and confusing. They may include the following categories.

Preferred Shares

Preferred shares—also known as preference stock or shares—are a specific type of stock. People who hold preferred shares receive dividends on their investment before the holders of common stock get a nickel. But preferred shares typically carry a fixed dividend, so (in public companies) their price doesn't fluctuate as much as the price of common shares. Investors who hold preferred shares may not receive the full benefit of a company's growth in value. When the company issues preferred shares, it sells them to investors at a certain initial price. The value shown on the balance sheet reflects that price.

Capital

The word *capital* means a number of things in business. *Physical capital* is plant, equipment, vehicles, and the like. *Financial capital* from an investor's point of view is the stocks and bonds he holds; from a company's point of view, it is the shareholders' equity investment plus whatever funds the company has borrowed. "Sources of capital" in an annual report shows where the company got its money. "Uses of capital" shows how the company used its money.

Most preferred shares do not carry voting rights. In a way, they're more like bonds than like common stock. The difference? With a bond, the owner gets a fixed coupon or interest payment; with preferred shares, the owner gets a fixed dividend. Companies use preferred stock to raise money because it does not carry the same legal implications as debt. If a company cannot pay a coupon on a bond, bondholders can force it into bankruptcy. Holders of preferred shares normally can't. Entrepreneurial companies often issue preferred shares to venture capital investors. These shares often have preferred payout rights senior to the common shares held by the original owners. If you take this route, make sure you understand the terms and conditions involved.

Common Shares or Common Stock

Common shares are the type of ownership shares that most small, non-public companies issue. This is probably what you and the other owners of your company hold. Unlike most preferred shares, common shares usually carry voting rights. People who hold them can vote for members of the board of directors (usually one vote per share) and on any other matter that may be put before the shareholders. Common shares may or may not pay dividends. The value shown on the balance sheet is typically shown at *par value*, which is the nominal dollar amount assigned to the stock by the issuer. Par value is usually a very small amount and has no relationship to the stock's actual value or market price. The balance sheet of our sample company (see appendix A) shows the common stock with a par value of $1.

Additional Paid-in Capital

Additional paid-in capital is the amount over the par value that investors initially paid for the stock. For example, if the stock is initially sold at $5 per share, and if the par value is $1 per share, the additional paid-in capital is $4 per share. It is summed up over time—so, for example, if a company issues additional shares, the additional paid-in capital is added to the existing amount.

Retained Earnings

Retained earnings, or accumulated earnings, are the profits that have been reinvested in the business instead of being paid out in dividends to the

Dividends

Dividends are funds distributed to shareholders taken from a company's equity. Public companies typically distribute dividends at the end of a quarter or year. Privately held companies can distribute them at any time, but many do it monthly or annually.

owners. The number represents the *total* after-tax income that has been reinvested or retained over the life of the business. Sometimes a company that holds a lot of retained earnings in the form of cash—Microsoft is one highly visible example—comes under pressure to pay out some of the money to shareholders, in the form of dividends. After all, what shareholder wants to see his money just sitting there in the company's coffers, rather than being reinvested in productive assets? Of course, you may see an accumulated deficit—a negative number—on the retained earnings line, which indicates that the company has lost money over time.

So owners' equity is what you and any other shareholders would receive if your company were sold, right? Of course not! Remember all those rules, estimates, and assumptions that affect the balance sheet. Assets are recorded at their acquisition price less accumulated depreciation. Goodwill is piled up with every acquisition the company makes, and it is never amortized. And of course, the company has intangible assets of its own, such as its brand name and customer list, which don't show up on the balance sheet at all. The moral: the market value of a company almost *never* matches its equity or book value on the balance sheet. The actual market value of a company is what a willing buyer would pay for it. In the case of a public company, that value is estimated by calculating the company's market cap, or the number of shares outstanding multiplied by the share price on any given day. In the case of private companies, the market value can be estimated by one of the valuation methods described in part 1—at least as a start.

11

Why the Balance Sheet Balances

If you learned in school about the fundamental accounting equation, the instructor probably said something like this: "It's called the balance sheet because it *balances*. Assets *always* equal liabilities plus owners' equity." But even if you dutifully wrote down that answer on the exam, you may be less than 100 percent clear on why the balance sheet balances. So here are three ways of understanding it.

REASONS FOR BALANCE

First, let's go back to an individual. You can look at a company's balance sheet in the same way you'd look at a person's net worth. Net worth has to equal what he owns minus what he owes because that's the way we define the term. The formulation of the equation for an individual, presented in chapter 8, is *owns – owes = net worth.* It's the same for a business. Owners' equity is defined as assets minus liabilities.

Second, look at what the balance sheet shows. On one side are the assets, which is what the company owns. On the other side are the liabilities and equity, which show how the company obtained what it owns. Since you can't get something for nothing, the "owns" side and the "how we obtained it" side will always be in balance. They have to be.

Third, consider what happens to the balance sheet over time. This approach should help you see why it always *stays* in balance.

Imagine a company that is just starting out. Its owner has invested $50,000 in the business, so he has $50,000 in cash on the assets side of the balance sheet. He has no liabilities yet, so he has $50,000 in owners' equity. The balance sheet balances.

Then the company buys a truck for $36,000 in cash. If nothing else changes—and if you constructed a balance sheet right after the truck transaction—the assets side of the balance sheet would look like this:

Assets	
Cash	$14,000
Property, plant, and equipment	36,000

It still adds up to $50,000—and on the other side of the balance sheet, he still has $50,000 worth of owners' equity. The balance sheet still balances.

Next imagine that the owner decides he needs more cash. So he goes to the bank and borrows $10,000, raising his total cash to $24,000. Now the balance sheet looks like this:

Assets	
Cash	$24,000
Property, plant, and equipment	36,000

Wow! It adds up to $60,000. The owner has increased his assets. But, of course, he has increased his liabilities as well. So the other side of the balance sheet looks like this:

Liabilities and Owners' Equity	
Bank loan	$10,000
Owners' equity	$50,000

That, too, adds up to $60,000.

Note that owners' equity remains unchanged throughout all these transactions. Owners' equity is affected only when a company takes in funds from its owners, pays out money to its owners, or records a profit or loss.

In the meantime, *every transaction that affects one side of the balance sheet affects the other as well.* For example:

- A company uses $100,000 cash to pay off a loan. The cash line on the assets side decreases by $100,000, and the liabilities line on the other side decreases by the same amount. So the balance sheet stays in balance.

- A company buys a $100,000 machine, paying $50,000 down and owing the rest. Now the cash line is $50,000 less than it used to be— but the new machine shows up on the assets side at $100,000. So total assets increase by $50,000. Meanwhile, the $50,000 owed on the machine shows up on the liabilities side. Again, we're still in balance.

As long as you remember the fundamental fact that transactions affect both sides of the balance sheet, you'll be OK. That's why the balance sheet balances. Understanding this point is a basic building block of financial intelligence. Remember, if assets don't equal liabilities and equity, there is incorrect data in your balance sheet. Start asking lots of questions.

12

The Income Statement Affects the Balance Sheet

So far we have been considering the balance sheet by itself. But here's one of the best-kept secrets in the world of financial statements: *a change in one statement nearly always has an impact on the other statements.* So when you're managing the income statement, you're also having an effect on the balance sheet.

THE EFFECT OF PROFIT ON EQUITY

To see the relationship between profit, from the income statement, and equity, which appears on the balance sheet, we'll look at a couple of examples. Here's a highly simplified balance sheet for a brand-new (and very small!) company:

Assets	
Cash	$25
Accounts receivable	0
Total assets	$25

Liabilities and Owners' Equity	
Accounts payable	$ 0
Owners' equity	$25

Say we operate this company for a month. We buy $50 worth of parts and materials, which we use to produce and sell $100 worth of finished product. We also incur $25 in other expenses. The income statement for the month looks like this:

Sales	$100
Cost of goods sold	50
Gross profit	50
All expenses	25
Net profit	$ 25

Now, what has changed on the balance sheet?

• First, we have spent all our cash to cover expenses.

• Second, we have $100 in receivables from our customers.

• Third, we have incurred $50 in obligations to our suppliers.

Thus, the balance sheet at the end of the month looks like this:

Assets	
Cash	$ 0
Accounts receivable	100
Total assets	$100

Liabilities and Owners' Equity	
Accounts payable	$ 50
Owners' equity	$ 50
Liabilities and owners' equity	$100

As you can see, that $25 of net profit becomes $25 of owners' equity. On a more detailed balance sheet, it would appear under "owners' equity" as retained earnings. That's true in any business: net profit increases equity unless it is paid out in dividends. By the same token, a net loss decreases equity. If a business loses money every month, liabilities will eventually exceed assets, creating negative equity. Then it is a candidate for bankruptcy court.

Note something else about this simple example: the company wound up that month with no cash! It was making money, and equity was growing, but it had nothing in the bank. So an entrepreneur needs to be aware of how both cash and profit interact on the balance sheet. This is a topic we'll return to in part 4, when we take up the cash flow statement.

AND MANY OTHER EFFECTS

The relationship between profit and equity isn't the only link between changes in the income statement and changes on the balance sheet. Far from it. Every sale recorded on the income statement generates an increase either in cash (if it's a cash sale) or in receivables. Every payroll dollar recorded as COGS or in operating expenses represents a dollar less on the cash line or a dollar more on the accrued-expenses line of the balance sheet. A purchase of materials adds to accounts payable, and so on. And of course, all these changes have an effect on total assets or liabilities.

Overall, if you tell your managers that their job is to boost profitability, they can have a positive effect on the balance sheet, just because profits increase equity. But it isn't quite so simple, because it matters how those profits are achieved, and it matters what happens to the other assets and liabilities on the balance sheet itself. For example:

- Your plant manager hears of a good deal on an important raw material and decides to buy a lot of it. Makes sense, right? Not necessarily. The inventory line on the balance sheet increases. The accounts payable line increases a corresponding amount. Eventually, the company will have to draw down its cash to cover the accounts payable—possibly long before the material is used to generate revenue. Meanwhile, your company has to pay to warehouse the inventory, and it may need to borrow money to cover the decrease in cash. Figuring out whether to take advantage of the deal requires detailed analysis; be sure to consider all the financial issues when making (or allowing your managers to make) these kinds of decisions.

- Your sales manager is looking to boost revenue and profit and decides to target smaller businesses as customers. Is it a good idea? Maybe not. Smaller customers may not be as good credit risks as larger ones. Accounts receivable may rise disproportionately because the customers are slower to pay. The accountant may need to increase that bad-debt allowance, which reduces profit, assets, and thus equity. The financially intelligent sales manager will need to investigate pricing possibilities: can he increase gross margin to compensate for the increased risk on sales to smaller customers?

- Your IT guy wants to buy a new computer system, believing that the new system will boost productivity and therefore contribute to profitability. But how is the new equipment going to be paid for? If your company is overleveraged—that is, if it has a heavy debt load compared with its equity—borrowing the money to pay for the system may not be a good idea. Perhaps you will need to take on additional equity investment in the company. When you make your decision about the computer system, you'll need to consider the best way to pay for it and its impact on your financial statements as well as the potential improvement in productivity.

Ideally, your managers would themselves be financially intelligent enough to step back now and then and look at the big picture. They would consider not just a line item on the income statement but the balance sheet as well (and the cash flow statement, which we'll get to shortly). If they can do this, they will be better managers—and will help you build a stronger company.

ASSESSING YOUR COMPANY'S HEALTH

Remember, we said at the beginning of this part that savvy investors typically pore over a company's balance sheet first. The reason is that the balance sheet answers a lot of questions—questions like the following:

- *Is the company solvent?* That is, do its assets outweigh its liabilities, so that owners' equity is a positive number?

- *Can the company pay its bills?* Here the important numbers are current assets, particularly cash, compared with current liabilities. More on this in part 5, on ratios.

- *Has owners' equity been growing over time?* A comparison of balance sheets for a period of time will show whether the company has been moving in the right direction.

These are simple, basic questions, of course. But they provide you with a deeper understanding of where your business stands than profit alone. Profit is important, and the data in the income statement helps you manage day to day. But company owners and other investors can learn much more from a detailed examination of the balance sheet and its footnotes, and from comparisons between the balance sheet and other statements. How important is goodwill to the company's "total assets" line? What assumptions have been used to determine depreciation, and how important is that? (Remember Waste Management.) Is the "cash" line increasing over time—usually a good sign—or is it decreasing? If owners' equity is rising, is that because the company has required an infusion of capital, or is it because the company has been making money?

The balance sheet, in short, helps show whether a company is financially healthy. All the statements help you make that judgment, but the balance sheet—a company's cumulative GPA—may be the most important of all.

If you would like to practice what you have learned (and give yourself another break from reading), please turn to the balance sheet exercise in appendix B.

Part Three
TOOLBOX

"EMPLOYEES ARE OUR MOST VALUABLE ASSET" (OR ARE THEY?)

Do you sometimes say, "Our people are our most valuable asset"? What exactly do you mean by that? Some big-company CEOs repeat that phrase as if it were a mantra but then cut expenses by letting people go. Can you imagine a company downsizing or laying off any other asset—just putting it out on the street in hopes that it will walk away?

From a commonsense perspective, employees *are* assets. Their knowledge and their work bring value to a company. When one company acquires another, the value of employees is recognized as part of the goodwill.

Otherwise, though, the value of employees doesn't show up on the balance sheet. There are two reasons:

- Outside of an acquisition, nobody has any idea how to value employees. What is the value of your top sales rep's knowledge? There isn't an accountant in the world who wants to tackle that one. And the Financial Accounting Standards Board, which makes the accounting rules for public companies, isn't about to take it on by amending GAAP.

- Anyway, companies don't own employees, so employees can't be considered assets in accounting terms.

Employees do create an expense: payroll, in one form or another, is often one of the biggest items on the income statement. But the phrase about employees being the most important assets has more to do with a company's culture and attitudes than it does with accounting. Some organizations really do seem to regard employees as assets. These companies train their people, invest in them, and take good care of them. Other companies focus on the expense angle, paying their people as little as they can and squeezing as much work out of them as possible. Is the former strategy worth it? Many people (including ourselves) believe that treating people right generally leads to higher morale, higher quality, and ultimately higher customer satisfaction. Other things being equal, it boosts the bottom line over the long term and thus increases a business's value. Of course, many other factors also influence whether a company succeeds or fails. So there's rarely a one-to-one correlation between a company's culture and attitudes (on the one hand) and its financial performance (on the other).

EXPENSE? OR CAPITAL EXPENDITURE?

When a company buys a piece of capital equipment, the cost doesn't show up on the income statement; rather, the new asset appears on the balance sheet, and only the depreciation appears on the income statement as a charge against profits. You might think the distinction between "expense" (showing up on the income statement) and "capital expenditure" (showing up on the balance sheet) would be clear and simple. But of course it isn't. Indeed, it's a prime canvas for the art of finance.

Consider that taking a big item off the income statement and putting it on the balance sheet, so that only the depreciation shows up as a charge against profits, can have the effect of increasing profits considerably. WorldCom is a case in point. A large portion of this big telecom company's expenses consisted of so-called line costs. These were fees it paid to local phone companies to use their phone lines. Line costs were normally treated as ordinary operating expenses, but you could argue (albeit incorrectly) that some of them were actually investments in new markets and wouldn't start paying off for years. That was the logic pursued by CFO Scott Sullivan, anyway, who began "capitalizing" his company's line costs in the late 1990s. Bingo: these expenses disappeared from the income statement, and profits rose by billions of dollars. To Wall Street, it appeared that WorldCom was suddenly generating profits in a down industry—and no one caught on until later, when the whole house of cards collapsed.

WorldCom took an overaggressive approach toward capitalizing its costs and wound up in hot water. But some companies will treat the occasional questionable item as a capital expenditure just to pump up their earnings a little so that the bottom line looks better to lenders and potential investors. Does yours?

Part Four

Cash Is King

13

Cash Is a Reality Check

"**C**ompanies hit the skids for all sorts of reasons," wrote Ram Charan and Jerry Useem in *Fortune* in May 2002, a time when a lot of companies were hitting the skids, "but it's one thing that ultimately kills them: they run out of cash." Entrepreneurs know this all too well. As Chip Conley, CEO of Joie de Vivre Hospitality, told us, probably the two most important measures for the entrepreneur who is just starting out are cash flow and burn rate (the amount of cash you burn through to operate in a given period, usually a month). Even in a more mature company, cash remains a critical variable.

In the big-company world, boards of directors and outside analysts sometimes focus too heavily on the income statement or the balance sheet. But even in this world there is one investor who watches cash closely: Warren Buffett. The reason? "He knows cash is hard to fudge."[1]

Warren Buffett may be the single greatest investor of all time. His company, Berkshire Hathaway, has invested in scores of companies and achieved astonishing results. From January 1994 to January 2006, Berkshire Hathaway's Class A stock compiled an amazing compound annual growth rate of 15.1 percent; in other words, it rose an average of about 15 percent every year for ten years. How does Buffett do it? Many people have written books attempting to explain his investing philosophy and his analytical approach. But in our opinion it all boils down to just three simple precepts. First, he evaluates a business based on its long-term rather than

Owner Earnings

Owner earnings is a measure of the company's ability to generate cash over a period of time. We like to say it is the money an owner could take out of his business and spend, say, at the grocery store for his own benefit. Owner earnings is an important measure because it allows for the continuing capital expenditures that are necessary to maintain a healthy business. Profit and even operating cash flow measures do not. More about owner earnings in the toolbox at the end of this part.

its short-term prospects. Second, he always looks for businesses he understands. (This led him to avoid dot-com investments.) And third, when he examines financial statements, he places the greatest emphasis on a measure of cash flow that he calls owner earnings. Warren Buffett has taken financial intelligence to a whole new level, and his net worth reflects it. How interesting that, to him, cash is king.

WHY CASH IS KING

Let's look at that third element of the financial statements, cash, in more detail. Why target cash flow as a key measure of business performance? Why not just profit, as found on the income statement? Why not just a company's assets or owners' equity, as revealed by the balance sheet? We suspect Warren Buffett knows that the income statement and balance sheet, however useful, have all sorts of potential biases, a result of all the assumptions and estimates that are built into them. Cash is different. Look at a company's cash flow statement, and you are indirectly peering into its bank account. Today, though the dot-com bust and the financial-fraud revelations of the late 1990s and early 2000s are several years in the past, cash flow is once again the darling of Wall Street. It has become a prominent measure by which analysts evaluate public companies. But Warren Buffett has been looking at cash all along because he knows that it's the number least affected by the art of finance.

Entrepreneurs are like Warren Buffett, but it's often more through necessity than through deep understanding. They are the ones who have to meet the payroll every week and pay the bills every month. They know that money in the bank is what counts. At a minimum they look at the checking account every week (and maybe every day) to determine whether there is enough cash to keep going.

But entrepreneurs may feel daunted when it comes to looking at a formal cash flow statement. For one thing, the language in the statement is a little arcane. Charan and Useem in their article were advocating a simple antidote to financial fraud: a "detailed, easily readable cash-flow report" required to be given to the board, to employees, and to investors. Unfortunately, no one, to our knowledge, has taken up the suggestion. So we are left with conventional cash flow statements. Most of these, however detailed, are hard for a nonfinancial person to read, let alone understand.

But talk about an investment that pays off: if you take the time to understand the cash flow statement, you can cut right through a lot of the smoke and mirrors created by your accountant or bookkeeper. You can see how good a job you and your company are doing at turning profit into cash. You can spot early-warning signs of trouble, and you will know how to manage so that cash flow is healthy. It isn't enough just to look at your checkbook because you can't always see the difference between different kinds of cash—cash from operations versus cash from the proceeds of a loan, for example. The cash flow statement shows these differences. Cash is a reality check on a business's performance, and the cash flow statement reveals the reality.

One of us, Joe, learned about the importance of cash when he was a financial analyst at a small company early in his career. The company was struggling, and everyone knew it. One day the CFO and the controller were both out golfing and were unreachable. (This was in the days before everybody had a cell phone, which shows you how old Joe is.) The banker called the office and talked with the CEO. Evidently, the CEO didn't like what he was hearing from the banker and felt he had better talk to someone in accounting or finance. So he passed the call to Joe. Joe learned from the banker that the company's credit line was maxed out. "Given that tomorrow is payday," the banker said, "we're curious about what your plan is to cover payroll." Thinking quickly (as always), Joe replied, "Um—can I call you back?" He then did some research and found that a big customer owed the company a good deal of money and that the check—really—was in the mail. He told the banker this, and the banker agreed to cover payroll, provided Joe brought the customer's check to the bank the minute it arrived.

In fact, the check arrived that same day, but after the bank closed. So first thing the next morning, Joe drove to the bank, check in hand. He arrived a few minutes before the bank opened and noticed that a line had already formed. In fact, he saw that several employees from his company were already there, holding their paychecks. One of them accosted him and said, "So you figured it out too, huh?" "Figured what out?" Joe asked. The guy looked at him with something resembling pity. "Figured *it* out. We've been taking our paychecks to the bank every Friday first break we get. We cash 'em and then deposit the cash in our own banks. That way, we can make sure the checks don't bounce—and if the bank won't cash them, we can spend the rest of the day looking for a job."

That was one day Joe's financial intelligence took a big leap upward. He realized what Warren Buffett and experienced entrepreneurs already knew: cash keeps a company alive, and cash flow is a critical measure of its financial health. You need people to run the business—any business. You need a place of business, telephones, electricity, computers, supplies, and so on. And you can't pay for all these things with profits because profits aren't real money. Cash is.

14

Profit ≠ Cash
(and You Need Both)

Why is profit not the same as cash coming in? Some reasons are pretty obvious: cash may be coming in from loans or from investors, and that cash isn't going to show up on the income statement at all. But even operating cash flow, which we'll explain in detail later, in chapter 15, is not at all the same as net profit.

There are three essential reasons:

• *Revenue is booked at sale.* One reason is the fundamental fact that we explained in our discussion of the income statement. A sale is recorded whenever a company delivers a product or service. Ace Printing Company delivers $1,000 worth of brochures to a customer; Ace Printing Company records revenue of $1,000, and theoretically it could record a profit based on subtracting its costs and expenses from that revenue. But no cash has changed hands because Ace's customer typically has thirty days or more to pay. Since profit starts with revenue, it always reflects customers' promises to pay. Cash flow, by contrast, always reflects cash transactions.

• *Expenses are matched to revenue.* The purpose of the income statement is to tote up all the costs and expenses associated with generating revenue during a given time period. As we saw in part 2, however, those expenses may not be the ones that were actually paid during that time period. Some may have been paid for earlier (as with the start-up we mentioned that had to pay for a year's rent in advance). Most will be paid for later, when vendors' bills come due. So the expenses on the income statement do not reflect cash going out. The cash flow statement, however, always measures cash in and out the door during a particular time period.

• *Capital expenditures don't count against profit.* Remember the toolbox at the end of part 3? A capital expenditure doesn't appear on the income statement when it occurs; only the depreciation is charged against revenue. So a company can buy trucks, machinery, computers, and so on, and the expense will appear on the income statement only gradually, over the useful life of each item. Cash, of course, is another story: all those items are often paid for long before they have been fully depreciated, and the cash used to pay for them will be reflected in the cash flow statement.

You may be thinking that in the long run cash flow will pretty much track net profit. Accounts receivable will be collected, so sales will turn into cash. Accounts payable will be paid, so expenses will more or less even out from one time period to the next. And capital expenditures will be depreciated, so over time the charges against revenue from depreciation will more or less equal the cash being spent on new assets. All this is true to a degree—at least for a mature, well-managed company. But the difference between profit and cash can create all sorts of mischief in the meantime, especially for an entrepreneurial company. Entrepreneurial businesses, after all, may face periods of fluctuating sales. They may have to cope with the fact that one big customer pays its bills very slowly—or that one important vendor requires payment up front. All these can wreak havoc on an entrepreneur's cash flow, even if they don't much affect profitability.

PROFIT WITHOUT CASH

We'll illustrate the difference between profit and cash by comparing two start-up companies with dramatically different profit and cash positions.

Sweet Dreams Bakery is a new cookies-and-cakes manufacturer that supplies specialty grocery stores. The founder has lined up orders based on her unique home-style recipes, and she's ready to launch on January 1. We'll assume she has $10,000 cash in the bank, and we'll also assume that in the first three months her sales are $20,000, $30,000, and $45,000. Cost of goods are 60 percent of sales, and her monthly operating expenses are $10,000.

Just by eyeballing those numbers, you can see she'll soon be making a profit. In fact, the simplified income statements for the first three months look like this:

	January	February	March
Sales	$20,000	$30,000	$45,000
COGS	12,000	18,000	27,000
Gross profit	8,000	12,000	18,000
Expenses	10,000	10,000	10,000
Net profit	($ 2,000)	$ 2,000	$ 8,000

A simplified cash flow statement, however, would tell a different story. Sweet Dreams Bakery has an agreement with its vendors to pay for the ingredients and other supplies it buys in thirty days. But those specialty grocery stores that the company sells to? They're kind of precarious, and they take sixty days to pay their bills. So here's what happens to Sweet Dreams' cash situation:

• In *January*, Sweet Dreams collects nothing from its customers. At the end of the month, all it has is $20,000 in receivables from its sales. Luckily, it does not have to pay anything out for the ingredients it uses, since its vendors expect to be paid in thirty days. (We'll assume that the COGS figure is all for ingredients, because the owner herself does all the baking.) But the company does have to pay expenses—rent, utilities, and so on. So all the initial $10,000 in cash goes out the door to pay expenses, and Sweet Dreams is left with no cash in the bank.

• In *February*, Sweet Dreams still hasn't collected anything. (Remember, its customers pay in sixty days.) At the end of the month, it has $50,000 in receivables—January's $20,000 plus February's $30,000— but still no cash. Meanwhile, Sweet Dreams now has to pay for the ingredients and supplies for January ($12,000), and it has another month's worth of expenses ($10,000). So it's now in the hole by $22,000.

Can the owner turn this around? Surely, in March those rising profits will improve the cash picture! Alas, no.

- In *March*, Sweet Dreams finally collects on its January sales, so it has $20,000 in cash coming in the door, leaving it only $2,000 short against its end-of-February cash position. But now it has to pay for February's COGS of $18,000 plus March's expenses of $10,000. So at the end of March, it ends up $30,000 in the hole—a worse position than at the end of February.

What's going on here? The answer is that Sweet Dreams is growing. (Sound familiar?) Its sales increase every month, meaning that it must pay more each month for its ingredients. Eventually, its operating expenses will increase as well because the owner will have to hire more people. The other problem is the disparity between the fact that Sweet Dreams must pay its vendors in thirty days while waiting sixty days for receipts from its customers. In effect, it has to front the cash for thirty days—and *as long as sales are increasing, it will never be able to catch up unless it finds additional sources of cash.* As fictional and oversimplified as Sweet Dreams may be, this is precisely how profitable companies go out of business. It is one reason why so many small entrepreneurial companies fail in their first year. They simply run out of cash.

CASH WITHOUT PROFIT

But now let's look at another sort of profit/cash disparity.

Fine Cigar Shops is another start-up. It sells very expensive cigars, and it's located in a part of town frequented by businesspeople and well-to-do tourists. Its sales for the first three months are $50,000, $75,000, and $95,000—again, a healthy growth trend. Its cost of goods is 70 percent of sales, and its monthly operating expenses are $30,000 (high rent!). For the sake of comparison, we'll say it, too, begins the period with $10,000 in the bank.

So Fine Cigar's income statement for these months looks like this:

	January	February	March
Sales	$ 50,000	$75,000	$95,000
COGS	35,000	52,500	66,500
Gross profit	15,000	22,500	28,500
Expenses	30,000	30,000	30,000
Net profit	($ 15,000)	($ 7,500)	($ 1,500)

Fine Cigar hasn't yet turned the corner on profitability, though it is losing less money each month. Meanwhile, what does its cash picture look like? As a retailer, of course, it collects the money on each sale immediately. And we'll assume that Fine Cigar was able to negotiate good terms with its vendors, paying them in sixty days.

- In *January*, it begins with $10,000 and adds $50,000 in cash sales. It doesn't have to pay for any cost of goods sold yet, so the only cash out the door is that $30,000 in expenses. End-of-the-month bank balance: $30,000.

- In *February*, it adds $75,000 in cash sales and still doesn't pay anything for cost of goods sold. So the month's net cash after the $30,000 in expenses is $45,000. Now the bank balance is $75,000!

- In *March*, it adds $95,000 in cash sales and pays for January's supplies ($35,000) and March's expenses ($30,000). Net cash in for the month is $30,000, and the bank balance is now $105,000.

Cash-based businesses—retailers, restaurants, and so on—can thus get an equally skewed picture of their situation. In this case Fine Cigar's bank balance is climbing every month even though the company is unprofitable. That's fine for a while, and it will continue to be fine so long as the company holds down expenses so that it can turn the corner on profitability. But the owner has to be careful: if he's lulled into thinking that his business is doing great and that he can increase those expenses, he's liable to continue on the unprofitable path. If he fails to attain profitability, *eventually he will run out of cash.*

Fine Cigar, too, has its real-world parallels. Every cash-based business, from tiny Main Street shops to giants such as Amazon.com and Dell, has the luxury of taking the customer's money before it must pay for its costs and expenses. It enjoys the float—and if it is growing, that float will grow ever larger. But ultimately, the company must be profitable by the standards of the income statement; cash flow in the long run is no protection against unprofitability. In the cigar-store example, the losses on the books will eventually lead to negative cash flow; just as profits eventually lead to cash, losses eventually use up cash. It's the timing of those cash flows that we are trying to understand here.

Understanding the difference between profit and cash is a key to increasing your financial intelligence, and it is critical for entrepreneurs. It opens a whole new window of opportunity to make smart decisions. For example:

- *Finding the right kind of expertise.* The two situations we described in this chapter require different skills. If a company is profitable but short on cash, then it needs financial expertise—someone capable of lining up additional financing. If a company has cash but is unprofitable, it needs operational expertise, someone capable of bringing down costs or generating additional revenue without adding costs. So financial statements tell you not only what is going on in the company; they also tell you what kind of expertise you need to hire. Many entrepreneurial companies aren't in a position to hire a full-fledged CFO in their first few years; an accountant retained on a transaction basis is sufficient to get the job done. But at some critical point—as in our scenarios—you will need to determine whether the company needs that full-time financial staff.

- *Making good decisions about timing.* Informed decisions on when to take an action can increase a company's effectiveness. Take Setpoint as an example. When Joe isn't out training people in business literacy, he is CFO of Setpoint, an entrepreneurial company that builds roller-coaster equipment and factory-automation systems. Managers at the company know that the first quarter of the year, when many orders for automation systems come in, is the most profitable for the business. But cash is always tight because Setpoint must pay out cash to buy components and pay contractors. The next quarter, Setpoint's cash flow typically improves because receivables from the prior quarter are collected, but profits slow down. Setpoint managers have learned that it's better to buy capital equipment for the business in the second quarter rather than the first, even though the second quarter is traditionally less profitable, just because there's more cash available to pay for it.

The ultimate lesson here is that companies need both profit and cash. They are different, and a healthy business, both in its early years and as it matures, requires both.

15

The Language of Cash Flow

When your business was just starting out, you may have received only an income statement from your accountant. The question you wanted answered was whether the company was profitable. Then your accountant told you that you needed a balance sheet to help you understand your company's assets and liabilities. That was fine. But ultimately, to see the full picture of your business, you also need a cash flow statement.

You'd think a cash flow statement would be easy to read. Since cash is real money, there are no assumptions and estimates incorporated in the numbers. Cash coming in is a positive number, cash going out is a negative one, and net cash is simply the sum of the two. In fact, though, we find that nearly every entrepreneur and nonfinancial manager takes a while to understand a cash flow statement. One reason is that it is always divided into categories, and the labels on the categories can be confusing. A second reason is that the positives and the negatives aren't always clear. For example, a typical line item might say, "(increase)/decrease in accounts receivable," followed by a positive or a negative number. Well, is it an increase or a decrease? A final reason is that it can be tough to see the relationship between the cash flow statement and the other two financial statements.

We'll take up the last issue in the following chapter. Right now, let's just sit down with a cash flow statement and learn the basic vocabulary.

TYPES OF CASH FLOW

The statement shows the cash moving into a business, called the inflows, and the cash moving out of a business, called the outflows. These are divided into three main categories.

Cash from or Used in Operating Activities

At times you'll see slight variations to the label, such as "cash provided by or used for operating activities." Whatever the specifics, it is more accountantspeak: too many accountants can't say "operations"; they have to say "operating activities." But whatever the exact language, this category includes all the cash flow, in and out, that is related to the actual operations of the business. It includes the cash customers send in when they pay their bills. It includes the cash the company pays out in salaries, to vendors, and to the landlord, along with all the other cash it must spend to keep the doors open and the business operating.

Cash from or Used in Investing Activities

The second category is called cash from or used in investing activities. Note that *investing activities* here refers to investments made by the company, not by its owners. The biggest subcategory here is cash spent on capital investments—that is, the purchase of assets. If the company buys a truck or a machine, the cash it pays out shows up on this part of the statement. Conversely, if the company sells a truck or a machine (or any other asset), the cash it receives shows up here.

Cash from or Used in Financing Activities

The final category is called cash from or used in financing activities. *Financing* refers to borrowing and paying back loans, on the one hand, and to transactions between a company and its shareholders, on the other. So if a company receives a loan, the proceeds show up in this category. If a company gets an equity investment from a shareholder, that too shows up here. Should the company pay off the principal on a loan, buy back its own stock, or pay a dividend to its shareholders, those expenditures of cash also would appear in this category.

You can see right away that there is a lot of useful information in the cash flow statement. The first category shows operating cash flow, which in many ways is the single most important number indicating the health of a business. A company with a consistently healthy operating cash flow is probably profitable, and it is probably doing a good job of turning its profits into cash. A healthy operating cash flow, moreover, means that it can finance more of its growth internally, without either borrowing or bringing in more outside investment.

The second category shows how much cash the company has spent on investments in its future. It reflects the idea that any successful business must make such investments. Printing companies need to buy presses and other equipment. Software development companies need high-powered computers. If the number in that second category is low relative to the size of the company, the owner may be treating the business as a cash cow, milking it for the cash it can generate while not investing in future growth. If the number is high, relatively speaking, it may suggest that the owner has high hopes for the future of the company. Of course, what counts as high or low will depend on the type of company it is. A service company, for instance, typically invests less in assets than a manufacturing company. So the analysis will vary according to the bigger picture of the company.

The third category shows to what extent the company is dependent on outside financing. Your cash flow statements over time will indicate whether your company is a net borrower (borrowing more than it is paying off). They'll also show whether you have been selling new shares to outside investors or buying back company stock.

Finally, the cash flow statement allows you to calculate Warren Buffett's famous "owner earnings" metric (see the toolbox at the end of this part).

We noted earlier that Wall Street in recent years has been focusing more and more on public companies' cash flow statements. As Warren Buffett knows, there is much less room for manipulation of the numbers on this statement than on the others. To be sure, "less room" doesn't mean "no room." For example, if a company is trying to show good cash flow in a particular quarter, it may delay paying vendors or employee bonuses until the next quarter. Unless a company delays payments over and over, however—and eventually, vendors who don't get paid will stop providing goods and services—the effects are significant only in the short term. All

Buying Back Stock

If a public company has extra cash and believes that its stock is trading at a price that is lower than it ought to be, it may buy back some of its shares. The effect is to decrease the number of shares outstanding so that each shareholder now owns a larger piece of the company. Privately held companies can also do stock buybacks—for example, when an owner or investor is bought out of the business. The price in this case would be negotiated by the parties involved, since there is no market-based share price for a private company.

this is true for private companies as well; it just doesn't show up on the public radar screen.

If your accountant hasn't put together a cash flow statement for you yet, ask him to. A cash flow statement, like the other two statements, is an important management tool for the business owner. So get one from your accountant, and then sit down with him and walk through the numbers together. Our guess is that it will be an eye-opening experience.

16

How Cash Connects
with Everything Else

Once you've learned to read the cash flow statement, you can inspect it for what it tells you about your company's cash situation, and you can then figure out how to improve your cash position. We'll spell out some of these opportunities in the following chapter.

But if you're the type of person who enjoys a puzzle—who likes to understand the logic of what you're looking at—then stick with us through this chapter. We will show you an interesting fact: *you can calculate a cash flow statement just by looking at the income statement and two balance sheets.* Now, this may not be what you thought you would be doing when you started your business, but hang in here. The information you'll learn by going through this exercise can be invaluable. It will certainly contribute to your understanding of how to get to what Gary Erickson, coleader of Clif Bar, calls your sweet spot. Among other things, that is when you are cash flow positive.

The calculations in this chapter aren't hard; they all require no more than adding and subtracting. But it's easy to get lost in the process. The reason is that accountants don't only have a special language and a special set of tools and techniques; they also have a certain way of thinking. They understand that profit as reported on the income statement is just the result of certain rules, assumptions, estimates, and calculations. They understand that assets as reported on the balance sheet aren't really worth what the balance sheet says, again because of the rules, assumptions, and estimates that go into valuing them. But accountants also understand that the art of finance, as we have called it, doesn't exist in the abstract. Ultimately, all those rules, assumptions, and estimates have to provide us with useful information about the real world. And since in finance the real world is represented by cash, the balance sheet and the income statement must have some logical relationship to the cash flow statement.

You can see the connections in common transactions. For example, remember that a credit sale worth $100 shows up both as an increase of $100 in accounts receivable on the balance sheet and as an increase of $100 in sales on the income statement. When the customer pays the bill, accounts receivable decreases by $100 and cash increases by $100 on the balance sheet. And because cash is involved, that same transaction affects the cash flow statement as well.

Remember, too, that when the company buys $100 worth of inventory, the balance sheet records two changes: accounts payable, or A/P, rises by $100 and inventory rises by $100. When the company pays the bill, A/P decreases by $100 and cash decreases by $100—again, both on the balance sheet. When that inventory is sold (either intact by a retailer or incorporated into a product by a manufacturer), $100 worth of cost of goods sold will be recorded on the income statement. Again, the cash part of the transaction will show up on the cash flow statement.

So all these transactions ultimately have an effect on the income statement, the balance sheet, and the cash flow statement. In fact, most transactions eventually find their way onto all three. To show you more of the specific connections, let us walk you through how accountants use the income statement and the balance sheet to calculate cash flow.

RECONCILING PROFIT AND CASH

The first exercise in this process is to reconcile profit to cash. The question you're trying to answer here is pretty simple: given that we have $X in net profit, what effect does that have on our cash flow?

We start with net profit for this reason: if every transaction were done in cash, and if there were no noncash expenses such as depreciation, net profit and operating cash flow would be identical. But since everything isn't a cash transaction, we need to determine which line items on the income statement and the balance sheet had the effect of increasing or decreasing cash—in other words, making operating cash flow *different* from net profit. As accountants put it, we need to find "adjustments" to net profit that, when added up, let us arrive at the changes in cash flow.

One such adjustment is in accounts receivable. We know that in any given time period, we're going to be taking in some cash from receivables, which will have the effect of decreasing the A/R line. We will also be making more credit sales, which will add to the A/R line. We can "net out" the cash figure from these two kinds of transactions by looking at the change in receivables from one balance sheet to the next. (Remember, the balance sheet is for a specific day, so changes can be seen when you compare two balance sheets.) Imagine, for example, we start with $100 in receivables on the balance sheet at the start of the month. We take in $75 in cash during the month, and we make $100 worth of credit sales. The new A/R line at the end of the month will be ($100 − $75 + $100) or $125. The change in receivables from the beginning of the period to the end is $25 ($100 − $125). It is also equal to new sales ($100) minus cash received ($75). Or to put it differently, cash received is equal to new sales minus the change in receivables.

Another adjustment is depreciation. Depreciation is deducted from operating profit on the way to calculating net profit. But depreciation is a noncash expense, as we have learned; it has no effect on cash flow. So you have to add it back in.

A START-UP COMPANY

Clear? Probably not. So let's imagine a simple start-up company, with sales of $100 in the first month. The cost of goods sold is $50, other expenses are

Reconciliation

In a financial context, reconciliation means getting the cash line on a company's balance sheet to match the actual cash the company has in the bank—sort of like balancing your checkbook, but on a larger scale.

$15, and depreciation is $10. You know that the income statement for the month will look like this:

Income Statement	
Sales	$100
COGS	50
Gross profit	50
Expenses	15
Depreciation	10
Net profit	$ 25

Let's assume that the sales are all receivables—no cash has come in yet—and COGS is all in payables. Using this information, we can construct two partial balance sheets:

Assets	Beginning of month	End of month	Change
Accounts receivable	0	$100	$100
Liabilities			
Accounts payable	0	$50	$50

Now we can take the first step in constructing a cash flow statement. The key rule here is that if an asset *increases*, cash *decreases*—so we subtract the increase from net income. With a liability, the opposite is true. If liabilities *increase*, cash *increases*, too—so we *add* the increase to net income.

Here are the calculations:

Start with net profit	$ 25
Subtract increase in A/R	(100)
Add increase in A/P	50
Add in depreciation	10
Equals: net change in cash	($ 15)

You can see that this is true because the only cash expense the company had during the period was $15 in expenses. With a real business, however, you can't confirm your results just by eyeballing them, so you need to calculate the cash flow statement according to the same rules.

A REALISTIC COMPANY

Let's try it with a more complex example. Here (for easy reference) are the income statement and balance sheets for the imaginary company whose financials appear in appendix A:

Income Statement *(in thousands)*

	Year ended Dec. 31, 2007
Sales	$8,689
Cost of goods sold	6,756
Gross profit	**$1,933**
Selling, general, and admin. (SG&A)	1,061
Depreciation	239
Other income	19
EBIT	**$ 652**
Interest expense	191
Taxes	213
Net profit	**$ 248**

Balance Sheet *(in thousands)*

	Dec. 31, 2007	Dec. 31, 2006
Assets		
Cash and cash equivalents	$ 83	$ 72
Accounts receivable	1,312	1,204
Inventory	1,270	1,514
Other current assets and accruals	85	67
Total current assets	2,750	2,857
Property, plant, and equipment	2,230	2,264
Other long-term assets	213	233
Total assets	**$5,193**	**$5,354**
Liabilities		
Accounts payable	$1,022	$1,129
Credit line	100	150
Current portion of long-term debt	52	51
Total current liabilities	1,174	1,330
Long-term debt	1,037	1,158
Other long-term liabilities	525	491
Total liabilities	**$2,736**	**$2,979**

Shareholders' equity

Common stock, $1 par value (100,000 authorized, 74,000 outstanding in 2007 and 2006)	$ 74	$ 74
Additional paid-in capital	1,110	1,110
Retained earnings	1,273	1,191
Total shareholders' equity	**$2,457**	**$2,375**
Total liabilities and shareholders' equity	**$5,193**	**$5,354**

2007 footnotes:

Depreciation	*$239*
Number of common shares (thousands)	*74*
Earnings per share	*$3.35*
Dividend per share	*$2.24*

The same logic applies as in the simple example we gave earlier:

• Look at every change from one balance sheet to the next.

• Determine whether the change resulted in an increase or a decrease in cash.

• Then add or subtract the amount to or from net income.

Here are the steps:

Observation	Action
Start with net profit, $248	
Depreciation was $239	Add that noncash expense to net profit
Accounts receivable increased by $108	Subtract that increase from net profit
Inventory declined by $244	Add that decrease to net profit
Other current assets rose by $18	Subtract that increase from net profit
PPE rose by $205 (after adjusting for depreciation of $239—see note 1)	Subtract that increase from net profit
Other long-term assets decreased by $20	Add that decrease to net profit

(*continued*)

Observation	Action
Accounts payable decreased by $107	Subtract that decrease from net profit
Credit line decreased by $50	Subtract that decrease from net profit
Current portion of long-term debt rose by $1	Add that increase to net profit
Long-term debt decreased by $121	Subtract that decrease from net profit
Other long-term liabilities increased by $34	Add that increase to net profit
Dividends paid—$166 (see note 2)	Subtract that payment from net profit

Note 1: Why do we need to adjust for depreciation when looking at the change in PPE? Remember that every year PPE on the balance sheet is lowered by the amount of depreciation charged to the assets in the account. So if you had a fleet of trucks that were acquired for $100,000, the balance sheet immediately after the acquisition would include $100,000 for trucks on the PPE line. If depreciation on the trucks was $10,000 for the year, then at the end of twelve months, the line in PPE for trucks would be $90,000. But depreciation is a noncash expense, and since we're trying to arrive at a cash number, we have to "factor out" depreciation by adding it back in.

Note 2: Notice the dividends footnoted on the balance sheet? Multiply the dividend by the number of shares outstanding, and you get roughly $166,000 (which we're representing as just $166). Net income of $248 minus the dividend of $166 equals $82—the precise amount by which shareholders' equity increased. This is the amount of profit that stayed in the company as retained earnings. If there is no dividend paid out or no new stock sold, then the cash provided or used by equity financing would be zero. Equity would simply increase or decrease by the amount of profit or loss in the period.

Now we can construct a cash flow statement based on all these steps (see following page). Of course, with a full balance sheet like this one, you have to put the change in cash in the right categories as well. The words in the right-hand column show where each number comes from. The "cash at end," of course, equals the cash balance on the ending balance sheet.

This is a complicated exercise! But you can see that there's a good deal of beauty and subtlety in all the connections (maybe only if you are an accountant). Go beneath the surface a little—or, to mix metaphors, read between the lines—and you can see how all the numbers relate to one another. Your financial intelligence is on the way up, as is your appreciation of the art of finance.

Cash Flow Statement *(in thousands)*

Year ended Dec. 31, 2007

Cash from operating activities

Net profit	$248	net profit on income statement
Depreciation	239	depreciation from income statement
Accounts receivable	(108)	change in A/R from 2006 to 2007
Inventory	244	change in inventory
Other current assets	(18)	change in other current assets
Accounts payable	(107)	change in A/P
Cash from operations	**$498**	

Cash from investing activities

Property, plant, and equipment	($205)	PPE change adjusted for depreciation
Other long-term assets	20	change from balance sheet
Cash from investing	**($185)**	

Cash from financing activities

Credit line	($50)	change in short-term credit
Current portion of long-term debt	1	change in current long-term debt
Long-term debt	(121)	change from balance sheet
Other long-term liabilities	34	change from balance sheet
Dividends paid	(166)	dividends paid to shareholders
Cash from financing	**($302)**	
Change in cash	11	add the three sections together
Cash at beginning	72	from 2006 balance sheet
Cash at end	**$ 83**	change in cash + beginning cash

17

Why Cash Matters

Of course, by now you may be saying to yourself, "So what? All this is cumbersome to figure out, and do I really need it?"

For starters, let's see what our sample company's cash flow statement reveals (that is, the cash flow statement for the imaginary company whose financials appear in the previous chapter and in appendix A). In terms of operations, it is certainly doing a good job of generating cash. Operating cash flow is considerably higher than net income. Inventory declined, so it's reasonable to suppose that the company is tightening up its operations. All this makes for a stronger cash position.

We can also see, however, that there is not a lot of new investment going on. Depreciation outweighed new investment, which makes us wonder whether management believes that the company has much of a future. Meanwhile, it is paying its shareholders a healthy dividend, which may suggest that they value it more for its current cash-generating abilities than for its future. (Many growing companies don't pay large dividends because they retain the earnings to invest in the business. Many, indeed, pay no dividends at all.) Of course, these are all suppositions; to really know the truth, you'd have to know a lot more about the company, what business it's in, and so on—the big-picture part of financial intelligence. But if you did know all those things, the cash flow statement would be extraordinarily revealing.

That brings us to your own company's cash flow. As an entrepreneur, you probably look at the check register every week or every month (or maybe every day, if that seat of your pants is getting thin). But here's why we said before that you need to understand the cash flow statement as well.

THE POWER OF UNDERSTANDING CASH FLOW

First, knowing your company's cash situation in detail will tell you not just whether the overall cash position is healthy but specifically where the cash is coming from. Is it from operations? That's a good thing—it means the business is generating cash. Is investing cash flow a sizable negative number? If it isn't, it may mean you aren't investing in the business—maybe not as much as your competitors or as much as your company needs for growth. To be sure, you probably know the needs of your business and what is going on in terms of capital expenditures, but watching the trend gives you an indication of where you have been and where you seem to be going. And what about financing cash flow? That category helps you track your indebtedness, and of course it reflects any stock transactions (such as selling shares to an outside investor) you may decide on. Looking at the cash flow statement tells you where your checkbook balance is coming from and which parts of your cash flow may need attention.

Second, you can do things to better your cash position. Consider, for example, a few of the things you can do to improve operating cash flow:

- *Accounts receivable.* Are you selling to customers who pay their bills on time? Do your salespeople, or you, have a close enough relationship with your customers to talk with them about payment terms? Do the people who answer the phone offer customers the kind of service that will encourage them to pay their bills on time? Is the product free of defects? Are the invoices accurate? Do the invoices go out on a timely basis? All these factors help determine how customers feel about your company and indirectly influence how fast they are likely to pay their bills. Disgruntled customers are not known for prompt payments—they like to wait until any dispute is resolved.

- *Inventory.* If you run a manufacturing company, do your engineers request special products all the time? If they do, they may be creating an inventory nightmare. If your operations people like to have lots in stock, just in case, they may be creating a situation in which cash is just sitting on the shelves, when it could be used for something else. Company owners and manufacturing managers can often reduce inventory hugely by studying and applying the principles of lean enterprise. Though lean techniques were pioneered at Toyota, plenty of small companies have learned to apply them effectively.

- *Expenses.* Do you defer expenses when you can? Do you consider the timing of cash flow when making purchases? Obviously, we're not saying it's always wise to defer expenses; it's just wise to understand what the cash impact will be when you do decide to spend money and to take that into account.

- *Giving credit.* Do you give credit to potential customers too easily? Alternatively, do you withhold credit when you should give it? Both decisions affect the company's cash flow and sales, which is why you and your credit manager or sales reps always have to strike a careful balance.

The list goes on. Maybe your plant manager is always recommending buying more equipment, just in case the orders come in. Perhaps whoever runs your IT system feels that the company always needs the latest upgrades. You have to respond to such requests, and every one will affect cash flow.

Third, entrepreneurs who understand cash flow tend to make better decisions day in and day out than those who focus purely on the income statement. In the following part, for instance, you'll learn to calculate ratios such as days sales outstanding, which is a key measure of a company's efficiency in collecting receivables. The faster receivables are collected, the better your company's cash position.

But our general point here is that cash flow is a key indicator of your company's financial health, along with profitability and shareholders' equity. It's the final link in the triad, and you need all three to assess how you are doing. It's also the final link in the first level of financial intelligence. You now have a good understanding of all three financial statements, so it's time to move on to the next level—to put that information to work.

Do you want to try reading and analyzing a cash flow statement? If you do—and we promise it is pretty straightforward—please turn to the cash flow statement exercise in appendix B.

Part Four
TOOLBOX

CASH ACCOUNTING

Often small start-up businesses do their accounting on a cash basis. A sale is recorded when the cash comes in. Costs are recorded as they are paid. In a cash-based business, increases or decreases in cash are the same as profit or loss. Not surprisingly, this approach is known as cash or cash-based accounting.

Cash-based accounting is a good, simple method when a business is in its infancy, or so long as it stays very small. As a business grows, however, cash-based accounting does not do a good job of matching revenue with costs (remember the matching principle). So nearly every growing business eventually adopts accrual accounting; it gives a more accurate picture of profits for a given period of time. You and your accountant need to determine when it makes sense to switch from cash to accrual.

FREE CASH FLOW

Although Wall Street probably isn't watching your company, part of your financial intelligence is understanding the context in which public companies operate. You can learn from the issues they are facing and the measures they are using to evaluate their performance. On that note, let's look at something called free cash flow.

EBITDA, as we noted earlier, is no longer Wall Street's favorite measure to watch. Now the hot metric is free cash flow. Some companies have looked at free cash flow for years. Warren Buffett's Berkshire Hathaway is the best-known example, though Buffett calls it owner earnings. As Buffett's term suggests, it's an important metric for entrepreneurial companies.

How to calculate free cash flow? First, get your cash flow statement. Next, take net cash from operations, and deduct the amount invested in capital equipment, as shown in the investment section of the statement. That's all there is to it—free cash flow is simply the cash generated by operating the business minus the money invested to keep it running. Once you think about it, it makes perfect sense as a performance measure. If you're trying to evaluate the cash your company generates, what you really want to know is the cash from the business itself minus the cash required to keep it healthy over the longer term.

Publicly traded companies are not required to disclose free cash flow, but most do report it, especially with the new Wall Street focus on cash. It might have helped us all back in the dot-com craze, when so many new companies had negative operating cash and huge capital investments. Their free cash flow was a big negative number, and their cash needs were covered only because investors were throwing lots of dollars into the pot. Buffett, who was nearly alone back then in relying on free cash flow, never invested in any of those companies. What a surprise!

At any rate, if your company's free cash flow is healthy and increasing, you know at least the following:

- Your company has options. You can use free cash flow to pay down debt, buy a competitor, or increase salaries (including your own).

- You and your colleagues can focus on the business, not on making payroll or on raising additional funds.

- If you're contemplating a public offering, Wall Street is likely to look more favorably on your company than it would otherwise.

Ratios:
Learning What the
Numbers Are Really
Telling You

18

The Power of Ratios

The eyes may or may not be a window into the soul, as Immanuel Kant suggested, but ratios are definitely a window into a company's financial statements. They offer a quick shortcut to understanding what the financials are saying, no matter whether the company is a start-up, a small but growing company, a struggling midsize business, or a large, publicly held company. A Paine Webber analyst named Andrew Shore knew this and used his skill at analyzing ratios to tell the public about a fraudulently managed public company—Sunbeam, when it was run by the notorious CEO "Chainsaw Al" Dunlap. We've mentioned Sunbeam before in this book, but now we want to relate a few more of the sorry details.

Dunlap had arrived at Sunbeam in early 1997. By the time he got there, he already had a great reputation on Wall Street and a standard *modus operandi.* He would show up at a troubled company, fire the management team, bring in his own people, and immediately start slashing expenses by closing down or selling factories and laying off thousands of employees. Soon the company would be showing a profit because of all those cuts, even though it might not be well positioned for the longer term. Dunlap would then arrange for it to be sold, usually at a premium—which means that he was often hailed as a champion of shareholder value. Sunbeam's stock jumped more than 50 percent on the news that he had been hired as CEO.

At Sunbeam, everything went according to plan until Dunlap began readying the company for sale in the fourth quarter of 1997. By then, he had cut the workforce in half, from twelve thousand to six thousand, and the company was reporting strong profits. Wall Street was so impressed that Sunbeam's stock price had gone through the roof—which, as we noted earlier, turned out to be a major problem. When the investment bankers went out to sell the company, the price was so high that they had trouble identifying prospective buyers. Dunlap's only hope was to boost sales and earnings to a level that could justify the kind of premium a buyer would have to offer for Sunbeam's stock.

ACCOUNTING TRICKS

We now know that Dunlap and his CFO, Russ Kersh, used a whole bag of accounting tricks in that fourth quarter to make Sunbeam look far stronger and more profitable than it actually was. One of the tricks was a perversion of a technique called bill-and-hold.

Bill-and-hold is essentially a way of accommodating retailers who want to buy large quantities of products for sale in the future but put off paying for them until the products are actually being sold. Say that you have a small chain of toy stores, and you want to ensure that you have an adequate supply of Barbie dolls for the Christmas season. Sometime in the spring, you might go to Mattel and propose a deal whereby you'll buy a certain number of Barbies, take delivery of them, and even allow Mattel to bill you for them—but you won't pay for the dolls until the Christmas season rolls around and you start selling them. Meanwhile, you'll keep them in a warehouse. It's a good deal for you, because you can count on having the Barbies when you need them yet hold off paying for them until you have decent cash flow. It's also a good deal for Mattel, which can make the sale and record it immediately, even though it has to wait a few more months to collect the cash.

Dunlap figured that a variation on bill-and-hold was one answer to his problem. The fourth quarter was not a particularly strong period for Sunbeam, which makes a lot of products geared toward summer—gas grills, for example. So Sunbeam went to major retailers such as Wal-Mart and Kmart and offered to guarantee that they'd have all the grills they wanted for the following summer provided they did their buying in the middle of winter. They'd be billed immediately, but they wouldn't have to pay until spring, when they actually put the goods in the stores. The retailers were cool to the idea. They didn't have anywhere to keep all that stuff, nor did they want to bear the cost of storing the inventory through the winter. "No problem," said Sunbeam. "We'll take care of that for you. We'll lease space near your facilities and cover all the storage costs ourselves."

Supposedly, the retailers agreed to those terms, although an audit conducted after Dunlap was fired failed to turn up a complete paper trail. In any case, Sunbeam went ahead and reported an additional $36 million in sales for the fourth quarter based on the bill-and-hold deals it had initiated. The scam worked well enough to fool most analysts, investors, and even Sunbeam's board of directors, which in early 1998 rewarded Dunlap and other members of the executive team with lucrative new employment contracts. Although they had been on the job for less than a year, they received some $38 million in stock grants, based largely on the mistaken belief that the company had just had a stellar fourth quarter.

But Andrew Shore, an analyst who specialized in consumer products companies, had been following Sunbeam since Dunlap arrived and now was scrutinizing its financials. He noticed some oddities, like higher-than-normal sales in the fourth quarter. Then he calculated a ratio called *days sales outstanding* (DSO) and found that it was huge, far above what it ought to have been. In effect, it indicated that the company's accounts receivable had gone through the roof. That was a bad sign, so he called a Sunbeam accountant to ask what was going on. The accountant told Shore about the bill-and-hold strategy. Shore realized that Sunbeam, in effect, had already recorded a hefty chunk of sales that would normally appear in the first and second quarters. After discovering this bill-and-hold game and other questionable practices, he promptly downgraded the stock.

The rest, as they say, is history. Dunlap tried to hang on, but the stock plummeted and investors grew wary of what Sunbeam's financials were telling them. Eventually, he was forced out—and it all started because Andrew Shore knew enough to dig beneath the surface and find out what was really going on. Ratios such as DSO were a useful tool for Shore, as they can be for owners and others involved in entrepreneurial enterprises.

ANALYZING RATIOS

Ratios indicate the relationship of one number to another. People use them every day. A baseball player's batting average of .333 shows the relationship between hits and official at bats—one hit for every three at bats. The odds of winning a lottery jackpot, say 1 in 6 million, show the relationship between winning tickets sold (1) and total tickets sold (6 million). Ratios don't require any complex calculations. To figure a ratio, usually, you just divide one number by another and then express the result as a decimal or as a percentage.

Different people use different kinds of financial ratios in assessing a business. For example:

- Bankers and other lenders examine ratios such as debt-to-equity, which gives them an idea of whether a company will be able to pay back a loan.

- Company owners and their top managers watch ratios such as gross margin, which helps them be aware of rising costs or inappropriate discounting.

- Credit managers (or anybody else who decides whether to give credit to a new customer, and how much) assess potential customers' financial health by inspecting their quick ratio. The ratio gives them an indication of a customer's supply of ready cash compared with its current liabilities.

- Potential and current shareholders—not to mention would-be acquirers—look at ratios such as price-to-earnings or, for a private company, a given multiple of annual EBITDA. That helps them decide whether a company is valued high or low in comparison with similar companies.

In this part we'll show you how to calculate many such ratios. The ability to calculate them—to draw more information out of financial reports than the raw numbers alone tell you—is a mark of financial intelligence. We'll show you how to use them to boost your company's performance. As an entrepreneur, you will learn things from these ratios that you would never have known from just looking at the bottom line on your income statement, let alone the balance in the company's checking account. You can then use that information to lead the company in the direction you want it to go.

The power of ratios lies in the fact that the numbers in the financial statements by themselves don't reveal the whole story. Is net profit of $1 million a healthy bottom line for a company? Who knows? It depends on the size of the company, on what net profit was last year, on what net profit was expected to be this year, and on many other variables. If you ask whether a $1 million profit is good or bad, the only possible answer is the one given by the woman in the old joke. Asked how her husband was, she replied, "Compared to what?"

Ratios offer points of comparison and thus tell you more than the raw numbers alone. Profit, for example, can be compared with sales, or with total assets, or with the amount you and other shareholders have invested in the company. A different ratio expresses each relationship, and each gives you a way of gauging whether a $1 million profit is good news or bad news. As we'll see, many of the different line items on the financials are incorporated into ratios. Those ratios help you understand whether the numbers you're looking at are favorable or unfavorable.

What's more, the ratios themselves can be compared. For instance:

- You can compare ratios with themselves over time. Is profit relative to sales up or down this year? This level of analysis can reveal some powerful trend lines—and some big warning flags if the ratios are headed in the wrong direction.

- You can also compare ratios with what you projected. To pick just one of the ratios we'll be examining in this part, if your inventory turnover is worse than you expected it to be, you need to find out why.

- You can compare ratios with industry averages (check with your industry trade group or association). If you find that your company's key ratios are worse than those of your competitors, you definitely want to figure out the reason. To be sure, not all the ratio results we discuss will be similar from one company to another, even in the same industry. For most, there's a reasonable range. It's when the ratios get outside of that range, as Sunbeam's DSO did, that it's worth your attention.

There are four categories of ratios that owners, managers, and other stakeholders in a business typically use to analyze the company's performance: profitability, leverage, liquidity, and efficiency. We will give you examples in each category. Note, however, that many of these formulas can be tinkered with by the financial folks to address specific approaches or concerns. Tinkering of this sort doesn't mean that people are cooking the books, only that they are using their expertise to obtain the most useful information for particular situations (yes, there is art even in formulas). What we will provide are the foundational formulas, the ones you need to learn first. Each provides a different view—like looking into a house through windows on all four sides.

19

Profitability Ratios

The Higher the Better (Mostly)

Profitability ratios help you evaluate your company's ability to generate profits. There are dozens of them, a fact that helps keep financial folks busy. But here we are going to focus on just five. These are really the only ones most entrepreneurs need to understand and use. Profitability ratios are the most common of ratios. If you get these, you'll be off to a good start in analyzing your financial reports (or any other company's).

Before we plunge in, however, do remember the artful aspects of what we're looking at. Profitability is a measure of a company's ability to generate sales and to control its expenses. None of these numbers is wholly objective. Sales are subject to rules about when the revenue can be recorded. Expenses are often a matter of estimation, if not guesswork. Assumptions are built into both sets of numbers. So profit as reported on the income statement is a product of the art of finance, and any ratio based on those numbers will itself reflect all those estimates and assumptions. We don't propose throwing out the baby with the bathwater—the ratios are still useful—only that you keep in mind that estimates and assumptions can always change.

Now, on to the five profitability ratios that we promised you.

GROSS PROFIT MARGIN PERCENTAGE

Gross profit, you'll recall, is revenue minus cost of goods sold or cost of services. *Gross profit margin percentage*, often called gross margin, is simply gross profit divided by revenue, with the result expressed as a percentage. Look at the sample income statement in appendix A, which we'll use to calculate examples of all these ratios. In this case the calculation is as follows:

$$\text{gross margin} = \frac{\text{gross profit}}{\text{revenue}} = \frac{\$1,933}{\$8,689} = 22.2\%$$

Gross margin shows the basic profitability of your product or service itself, before expenses or overhead are added in. It tells you how much of every sales dollar you get to use in the business—22.2 cents in this example—and (indirectly) how much you must pay out in direct costs (COGS or COS), just to get the product produced or the service delivered. (COGS or COS is 77.8 cents per sales dollar in this example.) It's thus a key measure of a company's financial health. After all, if you can't deliver your products or services at a price that is sufficiently above cost to support the rest of your company, you don't have a chance of earning a net profit.

Gary Erickson, coleader of Clif Bar, considers gross margin the most important ratio for entrepreneurs to understand, and the one that is essential to take a business to the next level. "Our first product in the bakery was a cookie," he says. "We had to figure out the total cost of producing that cookie and price it accordingly—enough to make a profit, but not so high that people wouldn't buy it." His analysis of gross margin helped him do that.

Trend lines in gross margin are equally important because they indicate potential problems. IBM not long ago announced great sales numbers in one quarter—better than expected—but the stock actually dropped. Why? Analysts noted that gross margin was heading downward and assumed that IBM must have been doing considerable discounting to record the sales it did. In your company a negative trend in gross margin indicates one of two things (sometimes both). Either the business is under severe price pressure, and you or your sales reps are being forced to discount; or else your materials, labor, and other direct costs are rising, driving up COGS or COS. Gross margin thus can be a kind of early-warning light, indicating favorable or unfavorable trends in the marketplace. It can help you anticipate challenges before they materialize.

OPERATING PROFIT MARGIN PERCENTAGE

Operating profit margin percentage, or operating margin, is a more comprehensive measure of your company's ability to generate profit. Remember, operating profit or EBIT is gross profit minus operating expenses, so the level of operating profit indicates how well you are running your entire business from an operational standpoint. Operating margin is just operating profit divided by revenue, with the result expressed as a percentage:

$$\text{operating margin} = \frac{\text{operating profit (EBIT)}}{\text{revenue}} = \frac{\$652}{\$8,689} = 7.5\%$$

Operating margin is another key metric for a company owner to watch. It's a good indicator of how well you and your managers as a group are doing your jobs. A downward trend line in operating margin should be a flashing yellow light. It shows that costs and expenses are rising faster than sales, which is rarely a healthy sign. As with gross margin, it's easier to see the trends in operating results when you're looking at percentages rather than at raw numbers. A percentage change shows not only the direction of the change but also how great a change it is.

NET PROFIT MARGIN PERCENTAGE

Net profit margin percentage, or net margin, tells a company how much out of every sales dollar it gets to keep after *everything* else has been paid for—people, vendors, lenders, the government, and so on. It is also known as return on sales, or ROS. It's just net profit divided by revenue, expressed as a percentage:

$$\text{net margin} = \frac{\text{net profit}}{\text{revenue}} = \frac{\$248}{\$8,689} = 2.9\%$$

Net profit is the proverbial bottom line, so net margin is a bottom-line ratio. But net margin is highly variable from one industry to another. It is low in most kinds of retailing, for example. In some kinds of manufacturing, it can be relatively high. The best point of comparison for net margin is a company's performance in previous time periods and its performance relative to similar companies in the same industry. Managers in big corporations don't spend a lot of time thinking about net profit margin; they can't affect interest and taxes, the two key differences between operating profit margin and net profit margin. But you, as an owner, may spend lots of time thinking about both interest and taxes, and it is important for you to understand how much of your profit is going to those two items.

All the ratios we have looked at so far use numbers from the income statement alone. Now we want to introduce two different profitability metrics, which draw from both the income statement and the balance sheet.

RETURN ON ASSETS

Return on assets, or ROA, tells you what percentage of every dollar *invested* in the business was returned to you as profit. This measure isn't quite as intuitive as the ones we already mentioned, but the fundamental idea isn't complex. Every business puts assets to work: cash, facilities, machinery, equipment, vehicles, inventory, whatever. A manufacturing company may have a lot of capital tied up in plant and equipment. A service business may have expensive computer and telecommunications systems. Retailers may have a lot of inventory. All these assets show up on the balance sheet. The total assets figure shows how many dollars, in whatever form, are being utilized in the business to generate profit. ROA simply shows how effective the company is at using those assets to generate profit. It's a measure that can be used in any industry to compare the performance of companies of different size.

The formula (and sample calculation) is simply this:

$$\text{return on assets} = \frac{\text{net profit}}{\text{total assets}} = \frac{\$248}{\$5,193} = 4.8\%$$

ROA has another idiosyncrasy by comparison with the income statement ratios mentioned earlier. Tax considerations aside, it's hard for gross margin or net margin to be too high; you generally want to see them as high as possible. But ROA can be too high. An ROA that is considerably above the industry norm may suggest that the company isn't renewing its

Return on Investment

Why isn't ROI included in our list of profitability ratios? The reason is that the term has a number of different meanings. Traditionally, ROI was the same as ROA: return on assets. But these days it can also mean return on a particular investment. What is the ROI on that machine? What's the ROI on our training program? What's the ROI of our new acquisition? These calculations will be different depending on how people are measuring costs and returns. We'll return to ROI calculations of this sort in the following part.

asset base for the future—that is, it isn't investing in new facilities and equipment. If that's true, its long-term prospects will be compromised, however good its ROA may look at the moment. ROA is a key ratio for entrepreneurs: as your business grows, you need to be acutely aware of how you are investing for the future, and ROA can help you keep tabs on that. (In assessing ROA, however, remember that norms vary widely from one industry to another. Service and retail businesses require less in terms of assets than manufacturing companies; then again, they usually generate lower margins.)

Another possibility if ROA is very high is that a company's leaders are playing fast and loose with the balance sheet, using various accounting tricks to reduce the asset base and therefore making the ROA look better than it otherwise would. And since ROA is one of the measures that public-company investors look at, there is an incentive to do so. Enron, for instance, set up a host of partnerships partially owned by CFO Andrew Fastow and other executives and then "sold" assets to the partnerships. The company's share of the partnerships' profits appeared on its income statement, but the assets were nowhere to be found on its balance sheet. Enron's ROA was great, but Enron wasn't a healthy company.

RETURN ON EQUITY

Return on equity, or ROE, is a little different: it tells us what percentage of profit you make for every dollar of equity invested in the company.

Remember the difference between assets and equity: *assets* refers to what the company owns, and *equity* refers to its net worth as determined by accounting rules.

As with the other profitability ratios, ROE can be used to compare a company with its competitors (and, indeed, with companies in other industries). Still, the comparison isn't always simple. For instance, Company A may have a higher ROE than Company B because it has borrowed more money—that is, it has greater liabilities and proportionately less equity invested in the company. Is this good or bad? The answer depends on whether Company A is taking on too much risk or whether, by contrast, it is using borrowed money judiciously to enhance its return. That gets us into ratios such as debt-to-equity, which we'll take up in the following chapter.

At any rate, here are the formula and sample calculation for ROE:

$$\text{return on equity} = \frac{\text{net profit}}{\text{shareholders' equity}} = \frac{\$248}{\$2,457} = 10.1\%$$

From an outside investor's perspective, ROE is a key ratio. Depending on interest rates, an investor can probably earn 3 percent or 4 percent on a treasury bond, which is essentially a risk-free investment. So if someone is going to put money into your company—or if you're going to invest in somebody else's business—he or you will want a substantially higher return on the equity. ROE doesn't specify how much cash an investor will ultimately get out of a company, since that depends on the company's decision about dividend payments and on how much the stock price appreciates until he sells. But it's a good indication of whether the company is even capable of generating a return that is worth whatever risk the investment may entail.

Again, note one thing about all these ratios: the numerator is some form of profit, which is always an estimate. The denominators, too, are based on assumptions and estimates. The ratios are useful, particularly when they are tracked over time to establish trend lines. But we shouldn't be lulled into thinking that they are impervious to artistic effort.

20

Leverage Ratios

The Balancing Act

Leverage ratios show you how—and how extensively—your business or any other company is using debt. *Debt* is a loaded word for many people: it conjures up images of credit cards, interest payments, an enterprise in hock to the bank. But consider the analogy with home ownership. As long as a family takes on a mortgage it can afford, debt allows them to live in a house that they might otherwise never be able to own. What's more, homeowners can deduct the interest paid on the debt from their taxable income, making it even cheaper to own that house. So it is with a business: debt allows a company to grow beyond what its invested capital alone would allow and, indeed, to earn profits that expand its equity base. A business can also deduct interest payments on debt from its taxable income. In the financial world the word for debt is *leverage*. The implication of this term is that a business can use a modest amount of capital to build up a larger amount of assets through debt to run the business, just the way a person using a lever can move a larger weight than she otherwise could.

The term *leverage* is actually defined in two ways in business—*operating leverage* and *financial leverage*. The ideas are related but different. Operating leverage is the ratio between fixed costs and variable costs; increasing your operating leverage means adding to fixed costs with the objective of reducing variable costs. A retailer that occupies a bigger, more efficient store and a service company that installs a larger, more efficient computer system are both increasing their fixed costs. But they hope to reduce their variable costs, because the new collection of assets is more efficient than the old. These are examples of operating leverage. Financial leverage, by contrast, simply means the extent to which a company's asset base is financed by debt.

Leverage of either kind enables a company to make more money, but it also increases risk. The airline industry is an example of a business with high operating leverage (all those airplanes!) and high financial leverage (since most of the planes are financed through debt). The combination creates enormous risk, because if revenue drops off for any reason, the companies are not easily able to cut those fixed costs. That's pretty much what happened after September 11, 2001. The airlines were forced to shut down for a couple of weeks, and the industry lost billions of dollars in a short amount of time. (Most of them haven't done too well in the years since then, either.)

In a small entrepreneurial company, debt can be a big part of what owners think (and worry) about. Do we bootstrap the company, just relying on profits and our own investments to fuel the business? Or do we go into debt—and if so, how much debt and what kind? The answers will always depend partly on your tolerance for risk. Are you cautious by nature? Or are you more like the folks at ECCO, an entrepreneurial company in Boise, Idaho, that makes back-up alarms, light bars for emergency vehicles, and other products? "We've been profitable for twenty-three consecutive years now," said CEO Ed Zimmer. "It got a little dicey at times because we had a couple years of 60 percent growth. You know, we did it with leverage. Sometimes the Visa was maxed, and the American Express had a big balance on it."

Here we will focus only on financial leverage, and we'll look at just two ratios: debt-to-equity and interest coverage.

DEBT-TO-EQUITY

The debt-to-equity ratio is simple and straightforward: it tells how much debt the company has for every dollar of shareholders' equity. The formula and sample calculation (again, based on the financials of the imaginary company in appendix A) look like this:

$$\text{debt-to-equity ratio} = \frac{\text{total liabilities}}{\text{shareholders' equity}} = \frac{\$2,736}{\$2,457} = 1.11$$

(Note that this ratio isn't usually expressed in percentage terms.) Both of these numbers come from the balance sheet.

What's a good debt-to-equity ratio? As with most ratios, the answer depends on the industry. But many, many companies have a debt-to-equity ratio considerably larger than 1—that is, they have more debt than equity. Since the interest on debt is deductible from a company's taxable income, plenty of companies use debt to finance at least a part of their business. In fact, public companies with particularly low debt-to-equity ratios may be targets for a leveraged buyout, in which management or other investors use debt to buy up the stock.

As you have probably learned by now, bankers love the debt-to-equity ratio. They use it to help them determine whether to offer a company a loan. They know from experience what a reasonable debt-to-equity ratio is for a company of a given size in a particular industry (and, of course, they check out profitability, cash flow, and other measures as well). Knowing the debt-to-equity ratio of your own company and how it compares both with competitors and with what bankers are looking for is a handy gauge of whether it is wise to consider taking on more debt. If the ratio is high, raising more cash through borrowing could be difficult. So expansion could require more equity investment.

INTEREST COVERAGE

Bankers love interest coverage, too. It's a measure of the company's interest exposure—how much interest it has to pay every year—relative to how much it's making. The formula and calculation look like this:

$$\text{interest coverage} = \frac{\text{operating profit}}{\text{annual interest charges}} = \frac{\$652}{\$191} = 3.41$$

In other words, the ratio shows how easy it will be for the company to pay its interest. A ratio that gets too close to 1 is obviously a bad sign: most of a company's profit is going to pay off interest! A high ratio is generally a sign that the company can afford to take on more debt—or at least that it can make the payments.

What happens when either of these ratios heads too far in the wrong direction—that is, too high for debt-to-equity and too low for interest coverage? We'd like to think that the response of a business owner is always to focus on paying off debt to get both ratios back into a reasonable range. But financial artists—and some entrepreneurs can also be financial artists—often have different ideas. There's a wonderful little invention called an operating lease, for instance, which is widely used in the airline industry and others. Rather than buying equipment such as an airplane outright, a company leases it from an investor. The lease payments count as an expense on the income statement, but there is no asset and no debt related to that asset on the company's books. Some companies that are already overleveraged are willing to pay a premium to lease equipment just to keep these two ratios in the area that bankers and investors like to see. If you want to get a complete sense of another company's indebtedness, by all means calculate the ratios—but try to determine whether the company uses any debt-like instruments, such as operating leases, as well.

You can bet that when you go to the banker, she will ask you for these two ratios and more. When Joie de Vivre Hospitality was young, says founder Chip Conley, "I had to do a series of financial analyses for a lender to make sure they felt that their debt was well protected." You will have to do the same.

21

Liquidity Ratios

Can We Pay Our Bills?

Liquidity ratios tell you about your company's ability to meet all its financial obligations—not just debt but payroll, payments to vendors, taxes, and so on. These ratios are particularly important to small businesses because small businesses are often in most danger of running out of cash. The ratios are also important whenever a larger company encounters financial trouble. Not to harp on the airlines too much, but again they are a case in point. You can bet that in the years right after 2001, professional investors and bondholders were carefully watching the liquidity ratios of some of the larger airlines.

Again, we'll limit ourselves to two of the most common ratios.

CURRENT RATIO

The current ratio measures a company's current assets against its current liabilities. Remember from the balance sheet chapters (part 3) that *current* in accountantese generally means a period of less than a year. So current assets are those that can be converted into cash in less than a year; the figure normally includes accounts receivable and inventory as well as cash. Current liabilities are those that will have to be paid off in less than a year, mostly accounts payable and short-term loans.

The formula and sample calculation for the current ratio (using the figures from the imaginary company in appendix A) are as follows:

$$\text{current ratio} = \frac{\text{current assets}}{\text{current liabilities}} = \frac{\$2{,}750}{\$1{,}174} = 2.34$$

This is another ratio that can be both too low and too high. In most industries a current ratio is too low when it is getting close to 1. At that point, you are just barely able to cover the liabilities that will come due with the cash you'll have coming in. Most bankers aren't going to lend money to a company with a current ratio anywhere near 1. Less than 1, of course, is *way* too low, regardless of how much cash you have in the bank. With a current ratio of less than 1, you know you're going to run short of cash sometime during the next year unless you can find a way of generating more cash or attracting more from investors.

A current ratio is too high when it suggests to outside shareholders that the company is sitting on its cash. Microsoft, for example, had amassed a cash hoard of nearly $60 billion (yes, billion) until 2004, when it announced a one-time dividend of $32 billion to its shareholders. You can imagine what its current ratio was before the dividend! (And it was probably pretty darn good after the dividend, too.) Whatever their size, fast-growing entrepreneurial companies need to pay special attention to this ratio, just because cash flow is always a challenge of high growth. A current ratio well above 1 can reassure a business owner that things will be OK. If the ratio heads down toward 1, it is time to pay attention.

QUICK RATIO

The quick ratio is also known as the *acid test*, which gives you an idea of its importance. Here are the formula and calculation:

$$\text{quick ratio} = \frac{\text{current assets} - \text{inventory}}{\text{current liabilities}} = \frac{\$2{,}750 - \$1{,}270}{\$1{,}174} = 1.26$$

Notice that the quick ratio is the current ratio with inventory removed from the calculation. What's the significance of subtracting inventory? Nearly everything else in the current assets category is cash or is easily transformed into cash. Most receivables, for example, will be paid in a month or two, so they're almost as good as cash. The quick ratio shows how easy it would be for a company to pay off its short-term debt without waiting to sell off inventory or convert it into product. Any business that has a lot of cash tied up in inventory has to know that lenders and vendors will be looking at its quick ratio—and that they will be expecting it (in most cases) to be above 1.

22

Efficiency Ratios

Making the Most of Your Assets

Efficiency ratios help you evaluate how efficiently you are managing certain key balance sheet assets and liabilities.

The phrase *managing the balance sheet* may have a peculiar ring, especially since many company owners focus mainly on managing their business's checkbook, or at best the income statement. But think about it: the balance sheet lists assets and liabilities, and these assets and liabilities are always in flux. If you can reduce inventory or speed up collection of receivables, you will have a direct and immediate impact on your company's cash position. Efficiency ratios let you know how you're doing on just such measures of performance. (We'll have more to say on managing the balance sheet in part 7.)

INVENTORY DAYS AND INVENTORY TURNOVER

The first two ratios that we will discuss can be a little confusing. They're based on the fact that inventory flows through a company, and it can flow at a greater or lesser speed. Moreover, how fast it flows matters a lot. If you look at inventory as frozen cash, then the faster you can get it out the door and collect the actual cash, the better off you will be.

So let's begin with a ratio sporting the catchy name *days in inventory*, or DII. (It's also called *inventory days*.) Essentially, it measures the number of days inventory stays in the system. The numerator is average inventory, which is beginning inventory plus ending inventory (found on the balance sheet for each date) divided by 2. (Some companies use just the ending inventory number.) The denominator is cost of goods sold (COGS) per day, which is a measure of how much inventory is actually used in each day. Here are the formula and sample calculation based on the information for the imaginary company in appendix A:

$$\text{DII} = \frac{\text{average inventory}}{\text{COGS/day}} = \frac{(\$1{,}270 + \$1{,}514)/2}{\$6{,}756/360} = 74.2$$

(Financial folks tend to use 360 as the number of days in a year, just because it's a round number.) In this example, inventory stayed in the system for 74.2 days. Whether that's good or bad, of course, depends on the product, the industry, the competition, and so on.

Inventory turns, the other inventory measure, is a measure of how many times inventory turns over in a year. If every item of inventory was processed at exactly the same rate, inventory turns would be the number of times per year you sold out your stock and had to replenish it. The formula and sample calculation are simple:

$$\text{inventory turns} = \frac{360}{\text{DII}} = \frac{360}{74.2} = 4.85$$

In the example, inventory turns over 4.85 times a year. But what are we actually measuring here? Both ratios are a measure of how efficiently a company uses its inventory. The higher the number of inventory turns—or the lower the inventory days—the tighter your management of inventory and the better your cash position. So long as you have enough inventory on hand to meet customer demands, the more efficient you can be, the better. In 2006 Target had inventory turns of 6.30—a pretty good number for a big retailer. But Wal-Mart's turns were 7.84, even better. In the retail business, a difference in the inventory turnover ratio can spell the difference between success and failure; both Target and Wal-Mart are successful, though Wal-Mart is certainly in the lead. If your company has a significant amount of inventory, you need to track these ratios carefully. They are key levers that can be used by financially intelligent entrepreneurs to build a more efficient organization.

DAYS SALES OUTSTANDING

Days sales outstanding, or DSO, is also known as *average collection period* and *receivable days*. It's a measure of the average time it takes to collect the cash from sales—in other words, how fast customers pay their bills.

The numerator of this ratio is ending accounts receivable, taken from the balance sheet at the end of the period you're looking at. The denominator is revenue per day—just the annual sales figure divided by 360. The formula and sample calculation look like this:

$$\text{days sales outstanding} = \frac{\text{ending A/R}}{\text{revenue/day}} = \frac{\$1,312}{\$8,689/360} = 54.4$$

In other words, it takes this company's customers an average of about fifty-four days to pay their bills.

DSO is a wonderful tool for entrepreneurs. That one number offers an avenue for rapid improvement in your company's cash position. Look at the sample company's number: it is taking a long time for customers to pay their bills. Customers are holding the cash that belongs to the company for an average of fifty-four days. If this were the case at your company, you would want to ask why is it taking so long. Are customers unhappy because of product defects or poor service? Are salespeople too lax in negotiating terms? Are they not following up with customers when an invoice hits its term (say, at thirty days)? Are invoices taking too long to reach the customer? Does the company need updated financial management software? DSO does tend to vary a good deal by industry, region, seasonality, and the state of the economy, but still: if this company could get its ratio down to forty-five or even forty days, it would improve its cash position considerably. This is a prime example of an important phenomenon, namely that careful management of basic administrative tasks—paperwork—can improve a business's financial picture even with no change in revenue or costs.

DSO is also a key ratio for anybody doing due diligence on a potential acquisition. A high DSO may be a red flag. Maybe the customers themselves are in financial trouble. Maybe the target company's operations and financial management are poor. Maybe, as was the case at Sunbeam, there is some fast-and-loose financial artistry going on. We'll come back to DSO in part 7, on the management of working capital; for the moment, note only that it is by definition a weighted average. So it's important that the due diligence looks at the aging of receivables—that is, how old specific invoices are and how many there are. It may be that a couple of unusually large, unusually late invoices are skewing the DSO number (see the toolbox for part 7).

DAYS PAYABLE OUTSTANDING

The *days payable outstanding* (DPO) ratio shows the average number of days it takes a company to pay its own outstanding invoices. It's sort of the flip side of DSO. The formula is similar: take ending accounts payable and divide by COGS per day:

$$\text{days payable outstanding} = \frac{\text{ending A/P}}{\text{COGS/day}} = \frac{\$1,022}{\$6,756/360} = 54.5$$

In other words, this company's suppliers are waiting a *long* time to get paid—about as long as the company is taking to collect its receivables.

So what? Isn't that the vendors' problem to worry about, rather than this company's owner or managers? Well, yes and no. The higher the DPO, the better a company's cash position, but the less happy its vendors are likely to be. A company with a reputation for slow payments may find that top-of-the-line vendors don't compete for its business quite as aggressively as they otherwise might. Prices might be a little higher, terms a little stiffer. A company with a reputation for prompt thirty-day payment will find the exact opposite. If you depend on your vendors for frequent deliveries, good prices, or access to the latest and greatest products, paying them within their terms helps you maintain good relationships—and that, in turn, helps ensure that your company will get what it needs. Watching DPO is a way of making sure that your company is sticking to whatever balance it wants to strike between preserving its cash and keeping vendors happy.

PROPERTY, PLANT, AND EQUIPMENT TURNOVER

Property, plant, and equipment turnover tells you how many dollars of sales your company gets for each dollar invested in property, plant, and equipment (PPE). It's a measure of how efficient you are at generating revenue from fixed assets such as buildings, vehicles, and machinery. The calculation is simply total revenue (from the income statement) divided by ending PPE (from the balance sheet):

$$\text{PPE turnover} = \frac{\text{revenue}}{\text{PPE}} = \frac{\$8,689}{\$2,230} = 3.90$$

By itself, $3.90 of sales for every dollar of PPE doesn't mean much, but it may mean a lot when compared with past performance and with competitors' performance. A company that generates a lower PPE turnover, other things being equal, isn't using its assets as efficiently as a company with a higher one. So check the trend lines and the industry averages to see how your company stacks up. (If you run a service company you may not have much PPE on your balance sheet, so this ratio won't tell you much about your business.)

At any rate, please note that sneaky little qualifier, "other things being equal." The fact is, this is one ratio where the art of finance can affect the numbers dramatically. If a company leases much of its equipment rather than owning it, for instance, the leased assets may not show up on its balance sheet. Its apparent asset base will be that much lower and its PPE turnover that much higher. A lease must meet specific requirements to qualify as an operating lease (which may not show up on the balance sheet) as opposed to a capital lease (which does). Check with your accountant before entering into any kind of lease to see what its effects will be.

TOTAL ASSET TURNOVER

Total asset turnover is the same idea as the previous ratio, but it compares revenue with total assets, not just fixed assets. (Total assets, remember, includes cash, receivables, and inventory as well as PPE and other long-term assets.) The formula and calculation:

$$\text{total asset turnover} = \frac{\text{revenue}}{\text{total assets}} = \frac{\$8,689}{\$5,193} = 1.67$$

Total asset turnover gauges not just efficiency in the use of fixed assets; it gauges efficiency in the use of all assets. If you can reduce inventory, total asset turnover rises. If you can cut average receivables, total asset turnover rises. If you can increase sales while holding assets constant (or increasing at a slower rate), total asset turnover rises. Any of these managing-the-balance-sheet moves improves efficiency and ultimately increases cash, so the ratio is important to a start-up. Watching the trends in total asset turnover shows you how you're doing.

There are many more ratios than these, of course. Financial professionals of all sorts use a lot of them. Investment analysts do, too. (A familiar one to public-company investors is the price-to-earnings ratio, which shows the relationship between a company's stock price and its earnings or profits.) Your own organization is likely to have specific ratios that are appropriate for the company, the industry, or both. You need to determine the ratios that are important in your business and then calculate and interpret them. That will provide plenty of information to help you decide how to address the financial status of your company. The ratios we have outlined here are the most common for most business owners.

Although understanding the financial statements is important, it is just a start on the journey to financial intelligence. Ratios take you to the next level; they give you a way to read between (or maybe underneath) the lines, so you can really see what is going on. They are a useful tool for analyzing your company and for telling its financial story.

Are you ready to practice pulling the three statements together and calculating some ratios? You'll learn a lot by doing it, rather than just reading about it. Please turn to the ratio exercise in appendix B.

Part Five
TOOLBOX

WHICH RATIOS ARE MOST IMPORTANT TO *YOUR* BUSINESS?

Certain ratios are generally seen as critical in certain industries. Retailers, for instance, watch inventory turnover closely. The faster they can turn their stock, the more efficient use they are making of their other assets, such as the store itself. But individual companies often like to create their own key ratios as well, depending on their circumstances and competitive situation. For example, Joe's company, Setpoint, is a small, project-based business that must keep a careful eye on both operating expenses and cash. So which ratios do Setpoint's managers watch most closely? One is home-grown: gross profit divided by operating expenses. Keeping an eye on that ratio ensures that operating expenses don't get out of line in comparison to the gross profit dollars the company is generating. The other is the current ratio, which compares current assets with current liabilities. The current ratio is usually a good indication of whether a company has enough cash to meet its obligations.

You may already have some key ratios that you watch closely. If not, think about what they might be. Ask your accountant and banker what numbers they study when they look at your business. Think about the numbers that keep you up at night and any others that tell you about the critical aspects of your business.

THE POWER OF PERCENT OF SALES

Is there a ratio built right into your company's income statement? Many companies do just that: they express each line item not only in dollars but as a percent of sales. For instance, COGS might be 68 percent of sales, operating expenses 20 percent, and so on. The percent-of-sales figure itself will be tracked over time to establish trend lines. Companies can pursue this analysis in some detail—for example, tracking what percent of sales each product line accounts for, or what percent of sales each store or region in a retail chain accounts for. The power here is that percent-of-sales calculations give a business owner and her managers much more information than the raw numbers alone. Percent of sales allows an operations manager, for example, to track his expenses in relationship to sales. Otherwise, it's tough for the manager to know whether he is in line as sales increase and decrease.

If your accountant doesn't break out percent of sales, try this exercise: locate your last three income statements, and calculate percent of sales for each major line item. Then track the results over time. If you see certain items creep up while others creep down, ask yourself why that happened—and if you don't know, dig deeper until you find out. The exercise can teach you a lot about where your operations can be improved. And next time you talk to your accountant, ask him to include that column in your income statement. For him, it is simply a matter of inserting the formula into the statement. For you, it is a powerful tool to improve your business.

SUSTAINABLE GROWTH RATE

Like the financial statements themselves, ratios fit together mathematically. We won't go into enormous detail here because this book isn't aimed at financial professionals. But one relationship among ratios is worth spelling out because it shows so clearly what we have been saying, namely that you and your managers can affect your business's ability to grow through internal financing by managing some key ratios.

In 1957 David Packard of Hewlett-Packard gave a landmark speech titled "Growth from Performance." In the speech Packard explained that HP was able to grow its revenue from $2.3 million in 1950 to $28 million in 1957 by maintaining some key ratios that supported this growth internally. This presentation led to a calculation that is now called the sustainable growth rate for a business.

The sustainable growth rate for a business is an estimate of the amount of growth a company can sustain without requiring outside equity investment.

The calculation is simple, even though it may not sound so. First, take a company's return on equity. Multiply that figure by the ratio of retained earnings to dividends. The result gives you the sustainable growth percentage that can be funded internally at current debt ratios.

To calculate return on equity, we are going to use the relationships among net profit margin, total asset turnover, and leverage (calculated as assets over equity) to show you the individual elements you can affect. Here's how to break down the process.

First, break down return on assets into the following:

$$\frac{\text{net income}}{\text{revenue}} \times \frac{\text{revenue}}{\text{assets}} = \frac{\text{net income}}{\text{assets}} = \text{ROA}$$

The first term, net income divided by revenue, is of course net profit margin percentage, or return on sales. The second term, revenue divided by assets, is asset turnover, discussed in chapter 22. Net profit margin multiplied by asset turnover equals ROA.

Then multiply the elements of ROA by assets/equity, and you will get return on equity (ROE). If you retain 100 percent of your earnings, ROE is your sustainable growth rate. Here is a summary of the relationship:

$$\frac{\text{net income}}{\text{revenue}} \times \frac{\text{revenue}}{\text{assets}} \times \frac{\text{assets}}{\text{equity}} = \text{ROE or sustainable growth rate}$$

This relationship assumes that you retain all your earning for growth. So let's say your net margin is 12 percent, your asset turnover is 1.50, and you have an equal amount of debt and equity in the business (so that the ratio of total assets to equity is 2). In this case, your sustainable growth percentage would be:

$12\% \times 1.50 \times 2 = 36\%$ (assuming you do not pay shareholder dividends)

The equation shows explicitly that there are three moves to the hoop, where the hoop is to increase your sustainable growth rate. One is to increase net profit margin, either by raising prices or by delivering goods or services more efficiently. That can be tough if the marketplace you operate in is highly competitive. A second is to increase the asset turnover ratio. That opens up another set of possible actions: reducing average inventory, reducing days sales outstanding, and reducing the purchase of property, plant, and equipment. Third, you can increase your ability to grow without giving up equity by increasing the use of debt. If you can't improve your net profit margin, working on the other two ratios—that is, managing the balance sheet—may be your best path to beating the competition and improving your sustainable growth rate.

How to Calculate (and Really Understand) Return on Investment

23

The Building Blocks of ROI

Financial intelligence is all about understanding how the financial side of business works and how financial decisions are made. The principles discussed in this chapter are the foundation of how some decisions—those relating to capital investment—are made in a business.

Most of us need little introduction to the fundamental principle of finance known as the *time value of money.* The reason is that we take advantage of it every day in our personal finances. We take out home mortgages and car loans. We run up big balances on our credit cards. When the debt gets too high, we refinance. Meanwhile, we're putting our own savings into interest-bearing checking or savings accounts, money-market funds, treasury bills, and stocks and bonds. Those of us who are entrepreneurs put some of our own money into a business, and we probably borrow money so that we can put still more into the business. We are a nation of borrowers, but we are also a nation of savers, lenders, and investors. Since all these activities reflect the time value of money, it's a safe bet that most of us have a gut-level understanding of the idea. Those who don't are likely to wind up on the losing end of the principle, which can be expensive indeed.

At its simplest, the principle of the time value of money says this: a dollar in your hand today is worth more than a dollar you expect to collect tomorrow—and it's worth a whole lot more than a dollar you hope to collect ten years from now. The reasons are obvious. You know you have today's dollar, whereas a dollar you expect to get tomorrow (let alone in ten years) is a little iffy. There's risk involved. What's more, you can buy something today with the dollar you have. If you want to spend the dollar you hope to have, you have to wait until you have it. Given the time value of money, anyone who lends money to somebody else expects to be paid interest, and anybody who borrows money expects to pay interest. The longer the time period and the higher the risk, the larger the interest charges are likely to be.

The principle is the same, of course, even if *interest* isn't the term used and even if there is no fixed expectation about what the return will be. Say your uncle Charlie buys stock in your software start-up. He's not going to get any interest on his investment, and he may never receive a dividend—but he hopes that the stock will eventually be worth far more than what he paid for it. In effect, he is lending your company money with the expectation of a return on his investment. When and if the return materializes, he can calculate it in percentage terms just as if it were really interest.

This is the basic principle that underlies a business's decisions about capital investments, which we will discuss in this part. The business has to spend cash that it has now in hopes of realizing a return at some future date. If you want to figure out whether it's worth buying a new machine or a new software application—tasks that we'll show you how to do in these pages—you will be relying on calculations that involve the time value of money.

FUTURE VALUE AND PRESENT VALUE

While the time value of money is the basic principle, the three key concepts you'll be using in analyzing capital expenditures are *future value*, *present value*, and *required rate of return*. You may find them confusing at first, but none of them is too complicated. They're simply ways to calculate the time value of money. If you can understand these concepts and use them in your decision making, you'll find yourself thinking more creatively—maybe we should say more artistically—about financial matters, just the way the pros do.

Future Value

Future value is what a given amount of cash will be worth in the future if it is loaned out or invested. In personal finance, it's a concept often used in retirement planning. Perhaps you have $50,000 in the bank at age thirty-five, and you want to know what that $50,000 will be worth at age sixty-five. That's the future value of the $50,000.

In the investment world, an analyst looking at public companies might project the value of a company's stock in two years if earnings grow at some given percentage a year. That future-value calculation can help her advise clients about whether the company is a good investment. In your company, you might be putting together a stock-option plan for key managers, and you might use future value to help determine the value of the stock in the future if you meet company goals.

Figuring future value offers a broad canvas for financial artists. Look at that retirement plan, for example. Do you assume an average 3 percent return over the next thirty years, or do you assume an average of 6 percent? The difference is substantial: at 3 percent your $50,000 will grow to slightly more than $121,000 (and never mind what inflation will have done to the value of a dollar in the meantime). At 6 percent it will grow to more than $287,000. It's tough to decide what's the right interest rate to use: how on earth can anyone know what interest rates will prevail over the next thirty years? At best, calculating future value that far out is educated guesswork—an exercise in artistry.

The stock analyst is in a somewhat better position because she is looking out only two years. Still, she has more variables to contend with. *Why* does she think earnings might grow at 3 percent or 5 percent or 7 percent or some other rate entirely? And what happens if they do? If earnings grow at only 3 percent, for instance, investors might lose interest and sell their shares, and the stock's price-to-earnings ratio might decline. If earnings grow at 7 percent, investors might get excited, buy more stock, and push up that ratio. And of course, the market itself will have an effect on the stock's price, and nobody can reliably predict the market's overall direction. Again, we're back to educated guesswork.

In fact, every calculation of future value involves a series of assumptions about what will happen between now and the time that you're looking at. Change the assumptions, and you get a different future value. The variance in return rates is a form of financial risk. The longer the investment outlook, the more estimating is required, hence the higher the risk.

Present Value

Present value is the concept used most often in capital expenditure analysis. It's the reverse of future value. Say you believe that a particular investment in growing your business will generate $100,000 in cash flow per year over the next three years. If you want to know whether the investment is worth whatever it is going to cost you, you need to know what that $300,000 would be worth right now. If the $300,000 payoff is worth (say) only $270,000 right now, you don't want to spend $275,000 on the investment.

Just as you use a particular interest rate to figure future value, you also use an interest rate to "discount" a future value and bring it back to present value. To take a simple example, the present value of $106,000 one year from now at 6 percent interest is $100,000. We are back to the notion that a dollar today is worth more than a dollar tomorrow. In this example, $106,000 next year is worth $100,000 today.

Present-value concepts are widely used to evaluate investments in equipment, real estate, business opportunities, and even mergers and acquisitions. But you can see the art of finance clearly here as well. To figure present value, you have to make assumptions *both* about the cash the investment will generate in the future *and* about what kind of an interest rate can reasonably be used to discount that future value.

Required Rate of Return

When you're figuring what interest rate to use in calculating present value, remember that you're working backward. You are assuming your investment will pay off a certain amount in the future, and you want to know how much is worth investing now to get that amount at a future date. So your decision about the interest or discount rate is essentially a decision about what interest rate you need to make the investment at all. You might not invest $100,000 now to get $102,000 in a year (a 2 percent rate), but you might very well invest $100,000 now to get $120,000 in a year (a 20 percent rate). Larger companies typically set a hurdle rate—the return they require before they will make the investment—but they typically set it higher for riskier projects than for less risky ones. Smaller companies like your own may not have an explicit hurdle rate, but you always have an implicit one;

after all, you will inevitably decide to make some investments and not others based on how much you expect the investments to return.

There is always some judgment involved in establishing a hurdle rate, but the judgment isn't wholly arbitrary. One factor is the opportunity cost involved. Your company, like any other, has only so much cash, and you have to make judgments about how best to use its funds. That 2 percent return is unattractive because you could do better just by buying a treasury bill, which might pay 3 percent or 4 percent with almost no risk. The 20 percent return may well be attractive—it's hard to make 20 percent on most investments—but it obviously depends on how risky the venture is. A second factor is your cost of capital. If you borrow money, you have to pay interest. If you use funds from equity investments in the business, your own or somebody else's, you and the other shareholders expect a return. The proposed investment has to add enough value to the company that debtholders can be repaid and the owners kept happy. An investment that returns less than the company's cost of capital won't meet these two objectives—so your hurdle rate should always be higher than the cost of capital.

That said, decisions about hurdle rates are rarely a matter of following a formula. You will have to evaluate how risky a given investment is, how it is likely to be financed, and what your company's overall situation is. You will have to determine whether the investment can generate a return at least comparable to what you can get elsewhere at a similar level of risk. You have to know how tight the company's cash position is, how much risk you are comfortable with, and what's going on in the marketplace you operate in. Then you have to make judgments—assumptions—about what

Opportunity Cost

In everyday language, this phrase denotes what you had to give up to follow a certain course of action. If you spend all your money on a fancy vacation, the opportunity cost is that you can't buy a car. In business, opportunity cost often means the potential benefit forgone from not following the financially optimal course of action.

kind of hurdle rate makes sense. High-growth companies typically use a high hurdle rate because they must invest their money where they think it will generate the level of growth they need. More stable, low-growth companies typically use a lower hurdle rate.

A word on the calculations involving these concepts: in the following chapter, we'll show you a formula or two. But you don't need to work it all out by hand; you can use a financial calculator, find a book of tables, or just go online. For instance, type "future-value calculator" into Google, and you'll get several sites where you can figure simple future values. To be sure, real-world calculations aren't always so easy. Maybe you think the investment you're considering will generate $100,000 in cash in the first year and 3 percent more in each of the subsequent years. Now you have to figure the increase, make assumptions about whether the appropriate discount rate should change from one year to the next, and so forth. If your company is big enough to have a CFO, he or she will do these calculations. Otherwise, you may want to seek help from your accountant or financial adviser. Usually, these finance professionals will have a spreadsheet or template with the appropriate formulas embedded, so that you or they can plug in the numbers. But you do have to be aware of the concepts and assumptions that they'll use in the process. If you're just plugging in numbers without understanding the logic, you won't understand why the results turn out as they do, and you won't know how to make them turn out differently by starting with different assumptions.

Cost of Capital

Financial analysts figure a company's cost of capital by (1) figuring the cost of its debt (the interest rate), (2) estimating the return expected by shareholders, and (3) taking a weighted average of the two. Say a company can borrow at 4 percent (after taking into account the fact that it can deduct interest payments from its taxes), and its shareholders expect a 16 percent return. Say it's financed 25 percent by debt and 75 percent by equity. The cost of capital is simply (25%)(4%) + (75%)(16%) = 13%. If an investment isn't projected to return more than 13 percent, it isn't likely to be funded.

We know plenty of entrepreneurs who get excited about an opportunity and who make decisions because it *feels* right. One of Joe's business partners, for instance, once proposed a significant capital investment. He asked Joe to do some analysis to confirm the decision. Joe replied that he was glad to do an analysis but asked what would happen if the analysis showed that the company shouldn't make the investment. His partner let him know that the analysis in that case would be wrong—he was sure the investment was needed. Joe declined to do the analysis just to justify a decision that was already made.

This is a common phenomenon: often people analyze investments only to justify them. We recommend that you do the analysis and take into account what it tells you before you decide to make capital investments in your business. That is financial intelligence in action.

So let's put these concepts to work.

24

Figuring ROI

The Nitty-Gritty

Capital expenditures. Cap-ex. Capital investments. Capital budgeting. And of course, return on investment, or ROI. Many companies use these terms loosely or even interchangeably, but they're usually referring to the same thing, namely the process of deciding what capital investments to make to improve the value of the company.

In most entrepreneurial companies, resources for capital expenditures are limited, and there's a lot of competition for what little is available. "This manager wants a new software application," says Paul Saginaw of Zingerman's, a specialty food company. "This manager wants a new mixer, this manager wants a new oven, and this manager wants a new POS [point-of-sale] system. In order to make good decisions among those choices, you have to learn how to evaluate the capital purchases you're going to make and what the returns on those investments are going to be, so that you are being a really good steward of the limited resources you have." That is precisely what this chapter is about.

ANALYZING CAPITAL EXPENDITURES

Capital expenditures are large projects that require a significant investment of cash. Every organization defines *significant* differently; some draw the line at $1,000, others at $5,000 or more. Capital projects are typically expected to help generate revenue or reduce costs for more than a year. The category is broad. It includes equipment purchases, business expansions, acquisitions, and the development of new products. A new marketing campaign can be considered a capital expenditure. So can the renovation of a building, the upgrade of a computer system, and the purchase of a new company car.

Expenditures like these are treated differently than ordinary purchases of inventory, supplies, utilities, and so on, for at least three reasons. One is simply that they require your company to commit large (and sometimes indeterminate) amounts of cash. A second is that they are typically expected to provide returns for several years, so the time value of money comes into play. A third is that they always entail some degree of risk. You may not know whether the expenditure will work—that is, whether it will deliver the expected results. Even if it does work as planned, you can't know exactly how much cash the investment will help generate. We will outline the basic steps of analyzing capital expenditures and then teach you the three methods finance people generally use for calculating whether a given expenditure is worth making.

But please, remember that this, too, is an exercise in the art of finance. It's actually kind of amazing: in larger companies, financial professionals can and do analyze proposed projects and make recommendations using a host of assumptions and estimates, and the results generally turn out well. They even enjoy the challenge of taking these unknowns and quantifying them in a way that makes their company more successful. With a little financial intelligence, you can do what they do. You may even want to involve some of the managers and employees who work for you. We know of an entrepreneurial company where the owners make a point of involving engineers and technicians in the capital budgeting process, precisely because they are likely to know more about what an investment in a steel-fabricating plant, say, will actually produce. The CFO of this company likes to say that he'd rather teach those people a little finance than learn metallurgy himself.

So here's how to go about it:

• Step 1 in analyzing a capital expenditure is to *determine the initial cash outlay.* Even this step involves estimates and assumptions: you must make judgments about what a machine or project is likely to cost before it begins to generate revenue. If Zingerman's is installing a new POS system, for instance, managers must consider not only the purchase price but also the costs of installation, of initial and ongoing training, of documenting the process, and of the turmoil in the business the new system will inevitably create. Typically, most of the costs are incurred during the first year, but some may spill over into year two or even year three. All these calculations should be done in terms of cash out the door, not in terms of decreased profits.

- Step 2 is to *project future cash flows* from the investment. (Again, you want to know cash inflows, not profit.) This is a tricky step—definitely an example of the art of finance—both because it is so difficult to predict the future and because there are many factors that need to be taken into account. (See the toolbox at the end of this part.) Business owners need to be conservative, even cautious, in projecting future cash flows from an investment. If the investment returns more than projected, everybody will be happy. If it returns significantly less, no one will be happy, and you may well have wasted your company's money.

- Step 3, finally, is to *evaluate the future cash flows*—to figure the return on investment. Are they substantial enough so that the investment is worth making? On what basis can we make that determination? Finance professionals typically use three different methods—alone or in combination—for deciding whether a given expenditure is worth it: the payback method, the net present value (NPV) method, and the internal rate of return (IRR) method. Each provides different information, and each has its characteristic strengths and weaknesses.

You can see right away that most of the work and intelligence in good capital budgeting involves the estimates of costs and returns. A lot of data must be collected and analyzed—a tough job in and of itself. Then the data has to be translated into projections about the future. Financially savvy entrepreneurs will understand that both of these are difficult processes and will examine their assumptions closely.

LEARNING THE THREE METHODS

To help you see these steps in action and understand how they work, we'll take a simple example. You're considering buying a $3,000 piece of equipment for your business—a specialized computer, say. It's expected to last three years. At the end of each of the three years, the cash flow from this piece of equipment is estimated at $1,300. You have decided that your required rate of return—the hurdle rate—should be 8 percent. Do you buy this computer or not?

Payback Method

The payback method is probably the simplest way to evaluate the future cash flow from a capital expenditure. It measures the time required for the cash flow from the project to return the original investment—in other words, it tells you how long it will take to get your money back. The payback period obviously has to be shorter than the life of the project; otherwise, there's no reason to make the investment at all. In our example, you just take the initial investment of $3,000 and divide by the cash flow per year to get the payback period:

$$\frac{\$3,000}{\$1,300/\text{year}} = 2.31 \text{ years}$$

Since we know the machine will last three years, the payback period meets the first test: it is shorter than the life of the project. What we have not yet calculated is how much cash the project will return over its entire life.

Right there you can see both the strengths and the weaknesses of the payback method. On the plus side, it is simple to calculate and explain. It provides a quick and easy reality check. If a project you are considering has a payback period that is obviously longer than the life of the project, you probably need to look no further. If it has a quicker payback period, you're probably justified in doing some more investigation. This is the method often used in meetings to quickly determine whether a project is worth exploring.

On the minus side, the payback method doesn't tell you much. A company doesn't want just to break even on an investment, after all; it wants to generate a return. This method doesn't consider the cash flow beyond breakeven, and it doesn't give you an overall return. Nor does the method consider the time value of money. The method compares the cash outlay today with projected cash flows tomorrow, but it is really comparing apples to oranges, because dollars today have a different value than dollars down the road.

For these reasons, payback should be used only to *compare* projects (so that you know which will return the initial investment sooner) or to *reject* projects (those that will never cover their initial investment). But remember, both numbers used in the calculation are estimates. The art in this is pulling the numbers together—how close can you come to quantifying an unknown?

So the payback method is a rough rule of thumb, not strong financial analysis. If your results with payback look promising, go on to the next method to see whether the investment is really worth making.

Net Present Value Method

The net present value method is more complex than payback, but it's also more powerful; indeed, it's usually the finance professional's first choice for analyzing capital expenditures. The reasons? One, it takes into account the time value of money, discounting future cash flows to obtain their value right now. Two, it considers a business's cost of capital or other hurdle rate. Three, it provides an answer in today's dollars, thus allowing you to compare the initial cash outlay with the present value of the return.

How to compute present value? As we mentioned, the actual calculation is usually part of a spreadsheet or template developed by whoever is helping you with the financial side of your company. You can also use a financial calculator, online tools, or the tables found in finance textbooks. But we'll show you what the actual formula—it's called the discounting equation—looks like, so you can look "underneath" the result and really know what it means.

The discounting equation looks like this:

$$PV = \frac{FV_1}{(1 + i)} + \frac{FV_2}{(1 + i)^2} + \cdots \frac{FV_n}{(1 + i)^n}$$

where:

PV = present value
FV = projected cash flow for each time period

i = discount or hurdle rate

n = number of time periods you're looking at

Net present value is simply equal to present value minus the initial cash outlay.

For the example we mentioned, the calculations would look like this:

$$PV = \frac{\$1,300}{1.08} + \frac{\$1,300}{(1.08)^2} + \frac{\$1,300}{(1.08)^3} = \$3,350$$

and

$$NPV = \$3,350 - \$3,000 = \$350$$

In words, the total expected cash flow of $3,900 is worth only $3,350 in today's dollars when discounted at 8 percent. Subtract the initial cash outlay of $3,000, and you get a net present value of $350.

How should you interpret this? If the net present value of a project is greater than zero, it should be accepted, because the return is greater than the company's hurdle rate. Here, the return of $350 shows you that the project has a return greater than 8 percent.

Sometimes you may want to run an NPV calculation using more than one discount rate. If you do, you'll see the following relationship:

• As the hurdle rate increases, NPV decreases.

• As the hurdle rate decreases, NPV increases.

This relationship holds because higher hurdle rates mean a higher opportunity cost for funds. If you set your hurdle rate at 20 percent, it means you're pretty confident you can get almost that much elsewhere for similar levels of risk. The new investment will have to be pretty darn good for you to decide to pry loose any funds. By contrast, if you can get only 4 percent elsewhere, many new investments may start to look good. Just as the Federal Reserve stimulates the national economy by lowering interest rates, you will tend to invest more if you have a lower hurdle rate. (Of course, it may not be wise policy to do so.)

One drawback of the net present value method is that it can be hard to explain and present to others—your management team, for instance, or your outside investors. Payback is easy to understand, but net present value is a number that's based on the *discounted value of future cash flows*. That's not a phrase that trips easily off the nonfinancial tongue. Still, if you want to use NPV, you should persist. Assuming that the hurdle rate is equal to or greater than your cost of capital, *any* investment that passes the net present value test will increase the company's value, and *any* investment that fails would (if carried out anyway) actually hurt the company and its shareholders.

Another potential drawback—the art of finance, again—is simply that NPV calculations are based on so many estimates and assumptions. The cash flow projections can only be estimated. The initial cost of a project may be hard to pin down. And different hurdle rates, of course, can give you radically different NPV results. Still, the more you understand about the method, the easier it will be to come up with assumptions that make sense. Your understanding of the analysis will allow you to confidently explain why, or why not, you are deciding to make the investment.

Internal Rate of Return Method

Calculating internal rate of return is similar to calculating net present value, but the variable is different. Rather than assuming a particular discount rate and then inspecting the present value of the investment, IRR calculates the actual return provided by the projected cash flows. That rate of return can then be compared with your hurdle rate to see whether the investment passes the test.

In our example, you are proposing to invest $3,000, and your business will receive $1,300 in cash flow at the end of each of the following three years. You can't just use the gross total cash flow of $3,900 to figure the rate of return because the return is spread out over three years. So we need to do some calculations.

First, here's another way of looking at IRR: it's the hurdle rate that makes net present value equal to zero. Remember, we said that as discount rates increase, NPV decreases. If you did NPV calculations using a higher and higher interest rate, you'd find NPV getting smaller and smaller until it finally turned negative, meaning the project no longer passed the hurdle rate. In the preceding example, if you tried 10 percent as the hurdle rate, you'd get an NPV of about $233. If you tried 20 percent, your NPV would be negative, at −$262. So the inflection point, where NPV equals zero, is somewhere between 10 percent and 20 percent. In theory, you could keep narrowing in until you found it. In practice, you can just use a financial calculator or a Web tool, and you will find that the point where NPV equals zero is 14.36 percent. That is the investment's internal rate of return.

IRR is an easy method to explain and present because it allows for a quick comparison of the project's return to the hurdle rate. On the downside, it does not quantify the project's contribution to the overall value of the company, as NPV does. It also does not quantify the effects of an important variable, namely how long the company expects to enjoy the given rate of return. When competing projects have different durations, using IRR exclusively can lead you to favor a quick-payback project with a high-percentage return when you should be investing in longer-payback projects with lower-percentage returns. IRR also does not address the issue of *scale*. For example, an IRR of 20 percent does not tell you anything about the dollar size of the return. It could be 20 percent of one dollar or 20 percent of one million dollars. NPV, by contrast, does tell you the dollar amount. When the stakes are high, in short, it may make sense to use both IRR and NPV.

COMPARING THE THREE METHODS

We've been hinting at two lessons here. One is that the three methods we have reviewed may lead you to make different decisions, depending on which one you rely on. The other is that the net present value method is the best choice when the methods conflict. Let's take another example and see how the differences play out.

Assume again that you want to invest $3,000 in computer equipment for the business. (Keeping the numbers small makes the calculations easier to follow.) Let's also imagine that there are three different possible investments in different types of computer systems, as follows:

• Investment A: returns cash flow of $1,000 per year for three years

• Investment B: returns cash flow of $3,600 at the end of year one

• Investment C: returns cash flow of $4,600 at the end of year three

Your required rate of return—the hurdle rate—is 9 percent, and all three investments carry similar levels of risk. If you could select only one of these investments, which would it be?

The payback method tells us how long it will take to get back the initial investment. Assuming the payback occurs at the end of each year, here is how it turns out:

- Investment A: three years

- Investment B: one year

- Investment C: three years

By this method alone, investment B is the clear winner. But if we run the calculations for net present value, here is how they turn out:

- Investment A: −$469 (negative!)

- Investment B: $303

- Investment C: $552

Now investment A is out, and investment C looks like the best choice. What does the internal rate of return method say?

- Investment A: 0 percent

- Investment B: 20 percent

- Investment C: 15.3 percent

Interesting. If we went by IRR alone, we would choose investment B. But the NPV calculation favors C—and that would be the correct decision. As NPV shows us, investment C is worth more in today's dollars than investment B.

The explanation? While B pays a higher return than C, it only pays that return for one year. With C we get a lower return, but we get it for three years. And three years at 15.3 percent is better than one year at 20 percent. Of course, if you assume you could keep on investing the money at 20 percent, then B would be better—but NPV can't take into account hypothetical future investments. What it does assume is that your company can go on earning 9 percent on its cash. But even so, if we take the $3,600 that investment B gives us at the end of year one and reinvest it at 9 percent, we still end up with less at the end of year three than we would get from investment C.

So it always makes sense to use NPV calculations for your investment decisions, even if you sometimes decide to use one of the other methods for discussion and presentation. But again, the most important step a business owner can take when analyzing capital expenditures is to revisit the cash flow estimates themselves. They are where the art of finance really comes into play and where entrepreneurs can make their biggest mistakes. Often it makes sense to do a *sensitivity analysis*—that is, check the calculations using future cash flows that are 80 percent or 90 percent of the original projections, and see whether the investment still makes sense. If it does, you can be more confident that your calculations are leading you to the right decision.

This chapter, we know, has involved a lot of calculating. But sometimes you'd be surprised at how intuitive the whole process can be. Not long ago, Joe was running a financial review meeting at Setpoint. A senior manager in the company was suggesting that Setpoint invest $80,000 in a new machining center so that it could produce certain parts in-house rather than relying on an outside vendor. Joe wasn't wild about the proposal for several reasons, but before he could speak up, a shop assembly technician asked the manager the following questions:

- Did you figure out the monthly cash flow return we will get on this new equipment? Eighty thousand dollars is a lot of money!

- Do you realize that we are in the spring and that the business is typically slow, and cash is tight, during the summer?

- Have you figured in the cost of labor to run the machine? We are all pretty busy in the shop; you will probably have to hire someone to run this equipment.

- Are there better ways we could spend that cash to grow the business?

After this grilling, the manager dropped the proposal. The assembly technician might not have been an expert in net present value calculations, but he sure understood the concepts.

Part Six
TOOLBOX

A STEP-BY-STEP GUIDE TO ANALYZING CAPITAL EXPENDITURES

You've been talking with your banker about getting a loan for a new piece of equipment for the plant, or maybe for a new marketing campaign. He's receptive, but he wants more data. "Sounds good," he says. "Write me up an ROI analysis. I'll look at it as soon as it's ready."

Don't panic. Here's a step-by-step guide to preparing your proposal:

1. Remember that ROI means return on investment—just another way of saying, "Prepare an analysis of this capital expenditure." The banker wants to know whether the investment will generate enough cash so that you can pay back the loan and still create value for your company.

2. Collect all the data you can about the cost of the investment. In the case of a new machine, total costs would include the purchase price, shipping costs, installation, factory downtime, debugging, and so on. Note where you must make estimates. Treat the total as your initial cash outlay. You will also need to determine the machine's useful life, not an easy task (but part of the art we enjoy so much!). You might talk to the manufacturer and to others who have purchased the equipment to help you answer that question.

3. Determine the benefits of the new investment, in terms of what it will save the company or what it will help the company earn. A calculation for a new machine should include any cost savings from greater output speed, less rework, a reduction in the number of people required to operate the equipment, increased sales because customers are

happier, and so on. The tricky part here is that you need to figure out how all these factors translate into an estimate of cash flow. Don't be afraid to ask for help from your accountant or financial adviser. Many finance professionals have been trained in this kind of thing, and they should be willing to help.

4. If you have determined a hurdle rate for your company, calculate the net present value of the project using this hurdle rate. If you haven't yet established a rate, decide on one. (It obviously needs to be higher than the interest rate on the loan you are applying for.)

5. Calculate payback and internal rate of return as well. You may get questions about what they are from your banker, so you need to have the answers ready.

6. Write up the proposal. Keep it brief. Describe the project, outline the costs and benefits (both financial and otherwise), and describe the risks. Discuss how it fits with your company's strategy or competitive situation. Include your NPV, payback, and IRR calculations in case there are questions about how you arrived at your results.

Business owners sometimes go overboard in writing up capital expenditure analyses. It's probably human nature: we all like new things, and it's usually pretty easy to make the numbers turn out so that the investment looks good. But we advise conservatism and caution. Explain exactly where you think the estimates are good and where you think they may be shaky. Do a sensitivity analysis, and show (if you can) that the estimate makes sense even if cash flows don't materialize at quite the level you hope. A conservative proposal is one that is likely to fly—and one that is likely to add the most to the company's value in the long run.

Applied Financial Intelligence: Working Capital Management

25

The Magic of Managing the Balance Sheet

We've mentioned the phrase *managing the balance sheet* a couple of times in this book. Right now, we want to go into greater detail about how to do it. The reason? Astute management of the balance sheet is like financial magic. It allows you to improve your company's financial performance even without boosting sales or lowering costs. Better balance sheet management makes a business more efficient at converting inputs to outputs and ultimately to cash. It speeds up the *cash conversion cycle*, a concept that we'll take up later in this part. Companies that can generate more cash in less time have greater freedom of action; they aren't so dependent on outside investors or lenders.

If your company is big enough to have a CFO and a finance department, they will have day-to-day responsibility for managing most of the balance sheet. They'll help you figure out how much to borrow and on what terms, help you line up equity investment when necessary, and generally keep an eye on the company's overall assets and liabilities. But any business owner, with or (especially) without a finance department, should understand the key concepts involved in managing the balance sheet. In particular, you need to understand the idea of managing *working capital*. Learn to help your people manage working capital better, and you will have a powerful effect on both your company's profitability and its cash position.

THE ELEMENTS OF WORKING CAPITAL

Working capital is a category of resources that includes cash, inventory, and receivables, minus whatever a company owes in the short term. It comes straight from the balance sheet, and it's often calculated according to the following formula:

working capital = current assets – current liabilities

Of course, this equation can be broken down further. Current assets, as we have seen, includes items such as cash, receivables, and inventory. Current liabilities includes payables and other short-term obligations. But these aren't isolated line items on the balance sheet; they represent different stages of the production cycle and different forms of working capital.

To understand this, imagine a small manufacturing company. Every production cycle begins with cash, which is the first component of working capital. The company takes the cash and buys some raw materials. That creates raw-materials inventory, a second component of working capital. Then the raw materials are used in production, creating work-in-process inventory and eventually finished-goods inventory, also part of the "inventory" component of working capital. Finally, the company sells the goods to customers, creating receivables, which are the third and last component of working capital (figure 25-1). In a service business, the cycle is similar but simpler. For example, our own company—the Business Literacy Institute—is partly a training business. Its operating cycle involves the time required to go from the initial development of training materials, to the completion of training classes, and finally to the collection of the bill. The more efficient we are in finishing a project and following up on collections, the healthier our profitability and cash flow will be. In fact, the best way to make money in a service business is to provide the service quickly and well and then to collect as soon as possible. Throughout this cycle, the *form* taken by working capital changes. But the *amount* doesn't change unless more cash enters the system—for example, from loans or from equity investments.

Of course, if the company buys on credit, then some of the cash remains intact—but a corresponding "payables" line is created on the liabilities side

FIGURE 25-1

Working capital and the production cycle

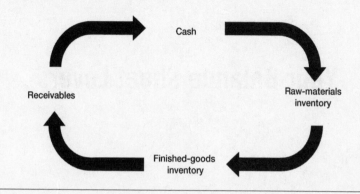

of the balance sheet. So that must be deducted from the three other components to get an accurate picture of the company's working capital.

Overall, how much working capital is appropriate for a company? This question doesn't have an easy answer. Every company needs enough cash and inventory to do its job. The larger it is and the faster it is growing, the more working capital it is likely to need. But the real challenge is to use working capital efficiently. The three working capital accounts that you and your employees can affect day in and day out are accounts receivable, inventory, and (to a lesser extent) accounts payable. We'll take up each one in turn.

Before we do, though, it's worth asking once again how much art is involved in all these calculations. In this case the best answer might be "some." Cash is a hard number, not easily subject to manipulation. Receivables and payables are relatively hard as well. Inventory isn't quite so hard. Various accounting techniques and assumptions allow a company to value inventory in different ways. So a company's calculation of working capital will depend to an extent on the rules its accountant follows. Still, you can generally assume that working capital figures aren't subject to as much discretion and judgment as many of the numbers we learned about earlier.

26

Your Balance Sheet Levers

Most companies use some of their cash to finance customers' purchase of products or services. That's the "accounts receivable" line on the balance sheet—the amount of money customers owe at a given point in time, based on the value of what they have purchased before that date.

The key ratio that measures accounts receivable, as we saw in part 5, is days sales outstanding, or DSO—that is, the average number of days it takes to collect on these receivables. *The longer a company's DSO, the more working capital is required to run the business.* Customers have more of the company's cash in the form of products or services not yet paid for, so that cash isn't available to buy inventory, deliver more services, and so on. Conversely, the shorter a company's DSO, the less working capital is required to run the business. It follows that the more people who understand DSO and work to bring it down, the more cash the company will have at its disposal.

MANAGING DSO

The first step in managing DSO is to understand what it is and in which direction it has been heading. If it's higher than it ought to be, and particularly if it's trending upward (which it nearly always seems to be), you need to begin asking questions.

Ask your operations manager, for example, whether there are any problems with the products or services that might make customers less willing to pay their bills. Is the company selling what customers want and expect? Is there a problem with delivery? Quality problems and late deliveries often provoke late payment, just because customers are not pleased with the products they're receiving and decide that they will take their own sweet time about payment. The people in production and shipping thus have an effect on receivables as well. In a service company, you need to be asking the same questions of the people who are out delivering the service. If service customers aren't satisfied with what they're getting, they too will take their time about paying.

Ask your customer-facing managers and employees—those in sales and customer service—a similar set of questions. Are our customers financially healthy? What is the standard in their industry for paying bills? Salespeople typically have the first contact with a customer, so it is up to them to flag any concerns about the customer's financial health. Once the sale is made, customer-service reps need to pick up the ball and learn what's going on. What's happening at the customer's shop? Are employees working overtime? Is the company laying people off? Meanwhile, salespeople need to work with the credit manager and customer service so that everybody understands the terms up front and will notice when a customer is late. At one company we worked with, the delivery people knew the most about customers' situations because they were at their facilities every day. They would alert sales and accounting if there seemed to be issues cropping up in a customer's business.

Chances are you have someone other than yourself reviewing the credit of customers and prospective customers. That person needs to ask whether the terms offered are good for the company and whether they fit the credit histories of the customers. He or she also needs to make judgments—maybe in consultation with you—about whether the company is giving credit too easily or whether it is too tough in its credit policies. There's always a trade-off between increasing sales on the one hand and issuing credit to poorer credit risks on the other. You and your sales or credit manager need to set the precise terms you're willing to offer. Is net thirty days satisfactory—or should you allow net sixty? You need to determine strategies such as offering discounts for early pay. For example, "2/10 net 30" means that customers get a discount of 2 percent if they pay their bill in ten days and no discount if they wait thirty days. Sometimes a 1 percent or 2 percent discount can help a struggling company collect its receivables and thereby lower its DSO—but of course, it does so by eating into profitability.

We know of a small company that has a simple, homegrown approach to the issue of giving credit to customers. The company has identified the traits it wants in its customers and has even named its ideal customer Bob. Bob's qualities include the following:

- He works for a large company.

- His company is known for paying its bills on time.

- He can maintain and understand the product provided (this company makes complex technology-intensive products).

- He is looking for an ongoing relationship.

If a new customer meets these criteria, it will get credit from this small manufacturer. Otherwise, it won't. As a result of this policy, the company has been able to keep its DSO quite low and to grow without additional equity investment.

All these decisions greatly affect accounts receivable and thus working capital. And the fact is, they can have a huge impact. Reducing DSO even by one day can save a company a lot of money. For example, check back to the DSO calculation in chapter 22, and you can calculate that one day of sales in our sample company is just over $24,000. Reducing DSO from fifty-five days to fifty-four in this company would thus increase cash by $24,000. That's cash that can be used for other things in the business.

MANAGING INVENTORY

Many business owners these days are focusing on inventory. They work to reduce inventory wherever possible. They are learning concepts such as *lean manufacturing*, *just-in-time inventory management*, and *economic order quantity*. The reason for all this attention is exactly what we're talking about here. Managing inventory efficiently reduces working capital requirements by freeing up large amounts of cash.

The challenge for inventory management, of course, isn't to reduce inventory to zero, which would probably leave a lot of customers unsatisfied.

The challenge is to reduce it to a minimum level while still ensuring that every raw material and every part will be available when needed and that every product will be ready for sale when a customer wants it. A manufacturer needs to be constantly ordering raw materials, making things, and holding those finished products for delivery to customers. Wholesalers and retailers need to replenish their stocks regularly to avoid the dreaded stockout—an item that isn't available when a customer wants it. Yet every item in inventory can be regarded as frozen cash, which is to say cash that the company cannot use for other purposes. Exactly how much inventory is required to satisfy customers while minimizing that frozen cash, well, that's the million-dollar question (and the reason for all that attention being paid to inventory).

The techniques for managing inventory are beyond the scope of this book. But we do want to emphasize that many different people in your company affect inventory levels, which means that all of them can have an impact on reducing working capital requirements. For example:

- Salespeople love to tell customers they can have exactly what they want. ("Have it *your* way," as the old Burger King jingle put it.) Custom paint job? No problem. Bells and whistles? No problem. Every variation, however, requires a little more inventory, meaning a little more cash. Obviously, customers must be satisfied. But that commonsense requirement has to be balanced against the fact that inventory costs money. The more that salespeople can sell standard products with limited variations, the less inventory their company will have to carry.

- Engineers love those same bells and whistles. In fact, they're constantly working to improve their company's products, replacing version 2.54 with version 2.55 and so on. Again, this is a laudable business objective, but it's one that has to be balanced against inventory requirements. A proliferation of product versions adds to frozen cash and puts a burden on inventory management. When a product line is kept simple with a few easily interchangeable options, the amount of inventory needed is likely to be less and therefore less cash is tied up.

- Production departments greatly affect inventory. For instance, what's the percentage of machine downtime? Frequent breakdowns require the company to carry more work-in-process inventory and more finished-goods inventory. And what's the average time between change-overs? Decisions about how much to build of a particular part have an enormous impact on inventory requirements. Even the layout of a plant affects inventory: an efficiently designed production flow in an efficient plant minimizes the need for inventory.

Along these lines, it's worth noting that many U.S. plants operate on a principle that eats up tremendous amounts of working capital. When business is slow, they nevertheless keep on churning out product with the goal of maintaining factory efficiency. Factory owners and plant managers focus on keeping unit costs down, often because they learned that goal early in their careers and no longer question it.

When business is good, the goal makes perfect sense: keeping unit costs down is simply a way of managing all the costs of production in an efficient manner. (This is the old approach of focusing only on the income statement, which is fine as far as it goes.) When demand is slow, however, the owner or plant manager must consider the company's cash as well as its unit costs. A plant that continues to turn out product in these circumstances is just creating more inventory that will sit on a shelf taking up space and cash. Coming to work and reading a book might be better than building product that is not ready to be sold.

How much can a company save through astute inventory management? Look again at our sample company: cutting just one day out of the DII number—reducing it from seventy-four days to seventy-three—would increase cash by nearly $19,000. Any company with inventory can save significant amounts of money, and thereby reduce working capital requirements, just by making modest improvements in its inventory management.

27

Homing In on
Cash Conversion

In this chapter we'll take up the cash conversion cycle, which measures how effectively a company collects its cash. But there's one little wrinkle we have to consider first—how fast a company decides to pay the money it owes its vendors.

Accounts payable is a tough number to get right. It's an area where finance meets philosophy. Financial considerations alone would encourage business owners to maximize days payable outstanding (DPO), thus conserving their company's cash. A change in this ratio is as powerful as a change in the other ratios we've been discussing. For instance, in the imaginary company we've looked at in many chapters now, if managers increased DPO by just one day, they would add about $19,000 to the company's cash balance.

But there are other considerations, as we mentioned in chapter 22. What kind of a relationship do you want with your vendors? What kind of reputation do you want? In practical terms, how much leverage do you have with your vendors—will they even continue doing business with your company if it is a late payer? Another practical consideration is the Dun & Bradstreet rating. D&B bases its scores, in part, on a company's payment history. An organization that consistently pays late may find that it has trouble getting a loan later on.

A personal story may illustrate the point. Joe's company, Setpoint, never lets an invoice go beyond thirty days. The company's philosophy is that slow payments simply aren't good business. Where did that philosophy come from? When Joe's partners, both engineers, started Setpoint, they had recently left another company. There, they had been project managers, designing custom products for the company's customers. But when they sent their designs out to be fabricated, nobody would build parts for them. When they asked why not, they found that their employer regularly took more than one hundred days to pay its bills. In effect, the engineers had to become negotiators just to get their projects built! When they started their own business, they vowed they would never put their new company's engineers in that position. While the philosophy puts constraints on cash flow, Setpoint's leaders believe that it positively affects the company's reputation and relationship with its vendors—and in the long term helps Setpoint build a stronger community of businesses around itself.

In general, if you notice that your company's DPO is climbing—and particularly if it is higher than your DSO—you might want to start asking a few questions. After all, the success of the company probably depends on good relationships with vendors, and you don't want to mess up those relationships unnecessarily.

THE CASH CONVERSION CYCLE

Another way to understand working capital is to study the cash conversion cycle. It's essentially a timeline relating the stages of production (the operating cycle) to the company's investment in working capital. The timeline has multiple levels, and you can see how the levels are linked in figure 27-1. Understanding these levels and their measures provides a powerful way of understanding your business and should help you make financially intelligent decisions.

Starting at the left, the company purchases raw materials. That begins the accounts payable period and the inventory period. In the next phase, the company has to pay for those raw materials. That begins the cash conversion cycle itself—that is, the cash has now been paid out, and the job is to see how fast it can come back. Yet the company is still in its inventory period; it hasn't actually sold any finished goods yet.

FIGURE 27-1

The operating cycle

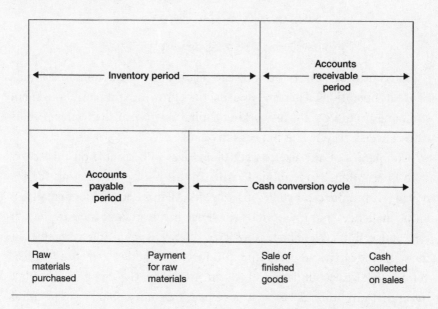

Eventually, the company does sell its finished goods, ending the inventory period. But it is just entering the accounts receivable period; it still hasn't received any cash. Finally, it does collect the cash on its sales, which ends both the accounts receivable period and the cash conversion cycle.

Why is this important? Because with it, we can determine how many days the cycle takes and then understand how many days a company's cash is tied up. That's an important number for company owners to know. Armed with the number, entrepreneurs may be able to find ways to "save" lots of cash for their company. To figure it out, use the following formula:

cash conversion cycle = DSO + DII – DPO

In other words, take days sales outstanding, add days in inventory, and subtract the number of days payable outstanding. That tells you, in days, how fast your company recovers its cash, from the moment it pays its payables to the moment it collects its receivables.

The cash conversion cycle also gives you a way of calculating how much cash it takes to finance the business: you just take sales per day and multiply it by the number of days in the cash conversion cycle. Here are the calculations for our sample company:

$$54 \text{ days} + 74 \text{ days} - 55 \text{ days} = 73 \text{ days}$$

$$73 \text{ days} \times \$24{,}136 \text{ sales/day} = \$1{,}761{,}928$$

This business requires working capital of around $1.8 million just to finance its operations. That isn't unusual for a growing company. Even small companies require a lot of working capital relative to their sales if their cash conversion cycle is as long as sixty days.

Companies of any size can get themselves into trouble on this score. Tyco International—mentioned earlier in this book—was famous for acquiring six hundred companies in two years. All those acquisitions entailed a lot of challenges, but one serious challenge involved huge increases in the cash conversion cycle. The reason? Tyco often was acquiring companies in the same industry, and competing products were added to its product list. With several very similar products in inventory, the company couldn't move that inventory as fast as it once had. Inventory days began to spiral out of control, increasing in some parts of the business by more than ten days. In a multinational company with more than $30 billion in revenue, increases on that scale can deplete cash by several hundred million dollars. (This is an issue that Tyco has addressed in recent years by closing down the acquisition pipeline and focusing on the operations of the business.)

The cash conversion cycle can be shortened by all the techniques discussed in this part: decreasing DSO, decreasing inventory, and increasing DPO. Figure out what your company's cycle is and which direction it's heading in. You may want to discuss it with your managers. That might start a conversation that will result in a faster cash conversion cycle, lower working capital requirements, and more cash. That will benefit everybody in the business.

Part Seven
TOOLBOX

WORKING WITH YOUR BANKER

The key element of working capital is cash, and if you don't have enough to finance your operations, you will need a loan. Many entrepreneurial companies, indeed, establish ongoing relationships with a bank and get loans regularly. One of the benefits of learning the material presented in this book is that you will be able to talk your banker's language. You'll be able to present the banker with a detailed analysis of your company's financial picture. You'll be able to show exactly why a loan makes financial sense and how you will repay it. You'll also be able to point out your financial strengths, identify your financial challenges, and discuss what you are planning to do about the latter.

When you apply for a loan, your banker will naturally want to see all the financial statements described in this book. In addition, he or she will probably want to see the following:

- A forecast of cash flow, sometimes for as much as twelve months. Any banker's primary concern is to know how a borrower plans to pay back the loan. And any business loan must be repaid out of cash flow. If you can show that your cash flow is healthy and likely to grow, you'll be that much more likely to get the money you need.

- A full-year budget, with updates and forecasts submitted monthly. Bankers also want to know what to expect about the business in general. They like to see a plan that shows projected sales, projected gross margin, and projected expenses. And they will want to know whether you are meeting your plan.

If you run into trouble along the way, don't hide it from your banker. Your problems will probably come out at some point anyway, and bankers hate surprises. "When we started out, I always thought bankers were our enemy," says Paul Saginaw, cofounder of Zingerman's, the specialty food company in Ann Arbor, Michigan. "We didn't want them knowing very much about what we were doing. But now I realize it's important to establish a good relationship with your bankers, and the sooner the better. Invite them into your business. Have them look at your annual plans and your budgeting and your forecasting so that they have a feel for it. The more they know about you, the better the job they're going to do when they bring your request to the loan committee.

"Besides," Saginaw adds, "at some point you're going to have tough times, and you're going to need money to get through. So you want your bankers armed with all the information they can possibly get so that they can confidently defend your business."

ACCOUNTS RECEIVABLE AGING

Want to manage accounts receivable more effectively? DSO is not the only measure to look at. Another is what's called the aging of receivables. Often, reviewing aging is the key to understanding the true situation in your company's receivables.

Here's why. As we mentioned earlier, DSO is by definition an average. For example, if you have $100,000 in receivables that are under ten days and $100,000 that are more than ninety days, your overall DSO is about fifty days. That doesn't sound too bad—but in fact, your company may be in substantial trouble because half of your customers don't seem to be paying their bills. Another business of the same size might have a DSO figure of fifty days with only $25,000 over ninety days. That business isn't in the same sort of trouble.

An aging analysis will present you with just these kinds of figures: total receivables under thirty days, total for thirty to sixty days, and so on. It's usually worth checking out that analysis as well as your overall DSO number to get the full picture of your receivables.

Creating a Financially Intelligent Company

28

Financial Literacy, Transparency, and Your Business's Performance

We have written this book in hopes of increasing your financial intelligence and helping you become a more effective leader. We firmly believe that understanding the financial statements, the ratios, and everything else we have included in the book will make you more effective as the chief executive of your own company. Frankly, we also think that understanding the financial side of the business will make entrepreneurship more meaningful. You would never play baseball or backgammon without first learning how the game is played; why should business be any different? Knowing the rules—how profits are figured, why return on assets matters so much, and all the rest—lets you see your entrepreneurial endeavors in the big-picture context of business enterprise, which is simply people working together to achieve certain objectives. You'll see more clearly how the company that you have started operates. You'll be able to assess your business's performance better than you could before because you can see which way the key numbers are moving and understand why they're moving in one direction or the other.

Then, of course, there's the fun of it. As we've shown, the financial report cards of business are partly reflections of reality. But they're also—sometimes very much so—reflections of estimates, assumptions, educated guesswork, and all the resulting biases. (Occasionally, they reflect outright manipulation as well.) Your accountant or CFO knows all this but probably hasn't done a good job of sharing that knowledge with you. Now you get to ask the finance types the tough questions. How do they recognize a particular category of revenue? Why did they choose a particular time frame for depreciation? Why is DII on the upswing? Of course, once they get past the shock of hearing that the boss speaks their language, they'll almost certainly be willing to discuss the bases for their assumptions and estimates and to modify them when appropriate. Who knows? The financial folks may even start asking for your advice about such matters.

BETTER COMPANIES

But we have another objective for this book as well. We also believe that businesses perform better when the financial intelligence quotient is higher among everybody—not just the owner but the managers and employees as well. A thriving business, after all, is a good thing. It offers valuable goods and services to its customers. It provides its employees with stable jobs, pay raises, and opportunities for advancement. It pays a healthy return to its owners. Overall, a prosperous business helps our economy grow, keeps our communities strong, and improves our standard of living.

Financially intelligent managers contribute to their companies' health because they can make better decisions. They can use their knowledge to help the company succeed. They manage resources more wisely, use financial information more astutely, and thereby increase their company's profitability and cash flow. They also understand more about why things happen and can lend their shoulder to the wheel instead of just carping about how misguided the owner or CEO is. We remember, for example, teaching a class of sales executives, using their company's actual financials. When we got to the cash flow statement—and showed them how the company's cash coffers had been drained to pursue growth by acquisition—one of the sales executives smiled. We asked him why he was smiling, and he laughed. "I've been fighting with the vice president of sales in my division for the better part of a year," he said. "The reason is, they changed our commission plan. We used to be paid on sales, and now we're paid when the sales are collected. Finally, I understand the reason for the change." He went on to explain that he agreed with the strategy of growth by acquisition, and he really didn't mind that the comp plan had been changed to support the strategy. He had just never understood the connection.

Financial intelligence makes for healthier business in another sense, too. A lot of companies today—even small ones—can be overcome by politics and power. They reward people who curry favor with their superiors and who build behind-the-scenes alliances. Common objectives get lost as individuals scurry to ensure their own advancement. At its worst, this kind of environment becomes toxic. At one company we worked with, employees thought that profit sharing was distributed only in years when employees complained loudly enough that they were unhappy. The purpose of profit sharing, they figured, was to keep them quiet. In reality, the company had a fairly straightforward plan that linked employees' efforts to their quarterly profit-sharing checks. But the politics were such that employees never believed the plan was real.

There's a simple antidote to politics: sunlight, transparency, and open communication. When everyone in the business understands the company's objectives and works to attain them, it's easier to create an organization built on a sense of trust and a feeling of community. *In the long run, that kind of organization will always be more successful than its less open counterparts.* Sure, an Enron or a WorldCom or a Sunbeam—not to mention their counterparts in the world of small business—can prosper for a while under secretive, self-serving leadership. But an organization that is successful over the long haul will almost invariably be built on trust, communication, and a shared sense of purpose. Financial training—an increase in financial intelligence—can make a big difference. At the company where employees thought that the purpose of profit sharing was to keep them quiet, those who underwent training learned how the plan really worked. Soon they were focusing their efforts on the numbers they affected—and soon they were getting a profit-sharing check every quarter.

Finally, financially savvy managers can react more quickly to the unexpected. There's a famous book called *Warfighting*, prepared by staff members of the U.S. Marine Corps, that was first published in 1989 and since then has become a bible of sorts for special forces of all kinds. One theme of the book is that marines in combat are always faced with uncertainty and rapidly changing conditions. They can rarely rely on instructions from above; instead they must make decisions on their own. So it's imperative that commanders spell out their broad objectives and then leave decisions about implementation to junior officers and ordinary marines in the field. That lesson is just as valuable to companies in today's mercurial business climate. Your managers probably have to make a lot of day-to-day decisions without consulting you or anybody else. If they understand the financial parameters they're working under, those decisions can be made more quickly and effectively. The company's performance—like the performance of a marine unit on the ground—will be that much stronger.

TAKING IT TO THE TROOPS

There's a next step here as well. If it makes a difference for managers to understand finance, imagine how much more of a difference it would make if everybody in a company understood it.

The same logic applies: people in offices, in stores and warehouses, on shop floors, and at client sites can make smarter decisions if they know something about how their part of the business is measured and about the financial implications of what they do every day. Should they rework a damaged part or use a new one? Should they work fast to get as much done as possible or work more deliberately to ensure fewer mistakes? Should they spend their time developing new services or cultivating and serving existing customers? How important is it to have everything a customer might possibly need? Like marines, frontline employees and supervisors should know the broad outlines of what the organization needs so that they can work smarter on the job.

Many companies understand this idea, of course, and in recent years have deluged employees and supervisors with performance goals, key performance indicators (KPIs), and other metrics. Maybe you have adopted some of these practices in your own business; if so, you know that there's typically a good deal of eye rolling and head shaking, particularly if the KPIs this quarter are different from last quarter's. But what if the folks in the field understood the financial logic of the KPIs or the performance goals? What if they understood that they are facing new KPIs this quarter not because you made some random decision but because the company's financial situation had changed? Like the sales executive in the class, most people are willing to adapt to a new situation provided they understand the reason for the change. If they don't understand, they may not know enough or care enough to do what the new situation requires.

Just as increasing your financial intelligence can boost your business's performance, so can financial intelligence among the troops. The Center for Effective Organizations, for instance, conducted a study that looked at (among other things) many measures of employee involvement.[1] Two measures in particular were "sharing information about business performance, plans and goals" and training employees in "skills in understanding the business." Both of these were positively related to productivity, customer satisfaction, quality, speed, profitability, competitiveness, and employee satisfaction. The more that organizations trained their people in financial literacy, in other words, the better the organizations did. Other students of management—including Daniel R. Denison, Peter Drucker, and Jeffrey Pfeffer—have studied and supported the idea that the more employees understand the business, the better the business performs. All these findings should come as no surprise. When people understand what's going on, the level of trust in the organization rises. Turnover drops. Motivation and commitment increase. Does anybody doubt that greater trust, motivation, and commitment lead to better performance?

One of us, Joe, has seen all these phenomena firsthand. He and his partners have spent years building a business, Setpoint, from the ground up. Like every start-up, it experienced periodic difficulties and crises, and more than once the company's accountant told Joe that it couldn't survive another period of turbulence. But somehow it always did. Finally, the accountant confessed to Joe, "You know, I think the reason why you get through these difficult times is because you train your employees and share the finances with them. When times are tough, the company rallies together and finds a way to fight through it."

The accountant was right: the employees all do know exactly where the company stands. Sharing financial information and helping subordinates and coworkers understand it is a way of creating a common purpose in a company. It fosters an environment where teamwork can survive and prosper.

So if you buy into this vision, what do you do? Short of sending all your employees out for financial training, is there anything you can do to help your company reach this state? Sure: do the training yourself. Teach some of the basics of finance to everyone. Introduce them to the artful aspects. Help them see the numbers as the useful tools they can be. Assist them in applying their knowledge on the job, every day.

Plenty of entrepreneurs have done this and have found that the investment of time is repaid in productivity and employee satisfaction. Most people like to learn, after all, particularly if they see the connection between the learning and how they can affect the company's results. The following chapter will offer some suggestions about how to teach them and how to make the learning stick. The toolbox at the end of this part provides an overview of a management philosophy based on financial literacy.

29

Financial Literacy Strategies

If your goal is to have a financially intelligent company, your first step is to figure out a strategy for getting there. We don't use the word *strategy* lightly. You can't just give a one-time training course, hand out an instruction book, or post the income statement and expect everyone to be enlightened. People need to be engaged in the learning. The material needs to be repeated and then revisited in different ways. Your results need to be shared. Financial literacy needs to become part of a company's culture. That takes time, effort, and even a little monetary investment. But it's very doable. We'll outline three approaches—ones that aren't mutually exclusive—that we have seen work.

TOOLS AND TECHNIQUES

The following tools and techniques hardly constitute an exhaustive list. But they are all approaches that you can implement on your own fairly easily.

Training (Over and Over)

Start by putting together three short training sessions. We don't mean anything fancy: even a PowerPoint presentation with some handouts works fine (though we would caution you that PowerPoint isn't always conducive to learning!). Each session should last between thirty and sixty minutes. Focus on one financial concept per session. Joe, for example, conducts three one-hour courses at Setpoint—on the income statement, on cash flow and project finance, and on the balance sheet. Depending on your situation, you might look at gross margin, selling expenses as a percent of sales, or even inventory turns. The concepts should be relevant to your business, and you should show people how they themselves affect the numbers.

Offer these classes *regularly*, maybe once a month. Let people attend two or three times if they want—it often takes that long for folks to get it. Encourage 100 percent attendance. Create an environment that tells participants that they are an important part of the business's success and that you want their involvement. Eventually, you can ask other people to teach the class—that's a good way for them to learn the material, and their teaching styles might be different enough from yours that they're able to reach people whom you can't.

Weekly "Numbers" Meetings

What are the two or three numbers that measure your company's performance week after week and month after month? What are the two or three numbers that you yourself watch? Shipments? Sales? Hours billed? Performance to budget? Chances are, the key numbers that you watch relate in some way to your company's financial statements and hence ultimately affect financial performance. So start sharing those numbers with your employees in weekly meetings. Explain where the numbers come from, why they're important, and how everybody affects them. Track the trend lines over time.

You know what will happen? Pretty soon people will begin talking about the numbers themselves. They'll start figuring out ways to move the needle in the right direction. Once that begins to occur, try taking it to the next level: *forecast* where the numbers will be in the coming month or quarter. You'd be amazed how people begin to take ownership of a number once they have staked their credibility on a forecast. (We've even seen companies where employees have set up a betting pool on where a given number will be!)

Reinforcements: Scoreboards and Other Visual Aids

It's fashionable these days for corporate executives to have a dashboard on their computers, showing where the business's performance indicators stand at any given moment. We always wonder why all companies, both small and large, don't have something similar out in the open for every employee to see. So not only do we recommend discussing the key number or numbers in meetings; we also suggest posting them on a scoreboard and comparing past performance with present performance and future forecasts. When the numbers are visible, it's tough for people to forget or ignore them. Remember, though, that small graphs can be easily ignored—and if they can be, they will be. As with your dashboard, make sure the scoreboard is clear, straightforward, and easy to see.

We also like visual aids that remind people how the company makes money. They provide a context for the day-to-day focus on key numbers. Our own company has developed what we call Money Maps, illustrating topics such as where profits come from. See the sample in figure 29-1: the map traces the entire business process at a fictional company, showing how much of each sales dollar goes to paying the expenses of each department,

FIGURE 29-1

Money map

Copyright © Business Literacy Institute. Illustrated by Dave Merrill.

and then highlighting how much is left over as profit. We customize these maps for our clients, so that everyone can see all of their own operations. But you can even draw maps and diagrams yourself. A visual is always a powerful tool for reinforcing learning. When people look at it, it reminds them how they fit into the big picture. It can have practical uses as well. One company we know of put up two copies of the same map. One copy showed the company's target numbers—what its best branch would do. On the other, managers wrote their own branch's numbers. People could see for each critical element how close they were to, or how far away from, the best branch's performance.

In all these approaches, you have to remember a few key precepts that have to do with the way adults learn. Probably the most important precept is to involve them in the learning. Adults learn least well if lectured to; they learn best if they are doing it themselves. So after you give them the basics, ask them to do the calculations, discuss the impact, and explain the meaning. We bet you'll hear some amazing things, like new ideas on how to reduce downtime or improve cash flow. Adults learn especially fast when they see a reason to. If they understand the big picture—and if they understand how what they're learning connects to their job, their impact on the company results, and their own financial situation (e.g., job security, the chance for raises)—they'll pay close attention. Just be careful not to make assumptions about what they already know. (Business owners often assume their employees know more about financial measurement than the employees really do.) Instead, teach those basics in a way that ensures no one is embarrassed about what they don't know. Keep the teaching tightly focused, keep it fun, and remember, don't try to make them into accountants!

In entrepreneurial companies, the "corporate culture" comes primarily from your philosophy about people, about communication, and about how a business should operate. If the culture is right in your company, the opportunity for improvement is huge. At one company we worked with, part of the education process included a change in language, which can be tremendously important in any culture change. It started at one location, where the regional manager began calling employees business partners. These new business partners took the change seriously, mostly because there were other things going on that reinforced the message, and began calling each other business partners. Before long they had even changed the parking lot signs, so that the word *employee* effectively disappeared from the location. Then other locations began to catch on, and soon the president of this national company was talking about business partners in the internal newsletter. The final piece came when a large customer wrote a thank-you to a vice president, calling the employees of this company business partners. The new language, in turn, was reflected in greater commitment, more involvement, and better results.

We know that it's hard to make this kind of change. It is a never-ending effort if it is to be successful. We just think that if the financials are out there and the key concepts repeatedly explained, every employee in the place will be more trusting and more loyal, and the company will be stronger for it. To be sure, publicly traded companies can't show consolidated financials to employees except once a quarter, when the information is released to the public. But they can certainly make a point of explaining those financials when they are released. In the meantime, they can make sure that employees see operating numbers for the department or facility they work in. Privately held companies, of course, don't face the same constraint. If you run a sole proprietorship or a closely held business, you have an advantage in that you can share as much information as you want to.

And don't be afraid to share information. Are you worried that competitors might use the information? Even if they did somehow get their hands on your income statement, they don't know what you are doing internally to get to those results. Or are you worried that employees will see the numbers and ask for a raise? More likely, employees assume the company is making more profit than it actually is. And when you talk about investments in the future of the business as well as returns to shareholders, they'll have an even better understanding of why all the leftover cash doesn't go to payroll.

You can see that we believe passionately in the power of knowledge—and when it comes to business, we believe most of all in the power of financial knowledge and the financial intelligence necessary to put it to work. Financial information is the nervous system of any business. It contains the data that shows how the business is faring—where its strengths are, where its weaknesses are, where its opportunities and threats are as well. For too long, a relative handful of people in each company were the only ones who understood what the financial data was telling them. We think more people should understand it. They'll be better off for gaining that understanding, and so will companies.

We also believe that you are in a unique position to build this kind of organization. As an entrepreneur, you have already shown that you are willing to take risks on new ideas. You are willing to do things in innovative ways. You depend on the enthusiasm and cooperation of your managers and employees, and financial literacy helps build both. Financial intelligence, in short, provides the foundation from which you can catapult your business to the next level. We hope that you do.

Putting Financial Intelligence to Work

Growing Your Business

Y ou'll have many opportunities, we suspect, to put the lessons you've learned in this book to practical use. For an example, consider one of the biggest issues that usually concerns company owners: whether, and how fast, to try growing the business.

Many entrepreneurs misunderstand the process of growth. They assume that all they have to do is create a profitable company, and growth will take care of itself. In reality, putting your company into a growth mode should be a conscious choice. Not every business owner decides to take that route. Some prefer running tiny operations, with no more than a few people on the payroll. Others choose to limit their growth even though they have opportunities to expand into midsize or large companies. (For some fascinating stories about companies that "chose to be great instead of big," see the book *Small Giants*, by Bo Burlingham.[1])

But if you do decide to pursue growth, you will find yourself facing a series of decisions and choices. For example, when should you add employees? How fast should you add them? Which skill sets do you need most urgently? Where and how will you look for candidates? Which candidate will you choose for each position? It can be tempting to make these decisions by the seat of your pants—hiring someone just because you need help right now, say, or because a friend has recommended someone who would be great for your business.

But hiring people always has big financial consequences. You are committed to paying those people's wages or salary unless and until you let them go. You will need enough cash on hand to make payroll every week or every month. You will have to abide by the laws and procedures governing personnel, such as gathering the required documentation from potential new employees and determining the requirements for workers' compensation insurance. You will have to withhold taxes (which usually means engaging a payroll-services firm), and you will have to factor payroll taxes into your budget. If the people you want to hire expect benefits such as health insurance, you will have to set up and pay for an insurance plan. And don't forget: everybody in a business needs workspace and equipment, whether it's a computer, a phone, tools, a uniform, or whatever.

All these prospective expenses must be factored into the hiring decision. Most can be costed out with a high degree of accuracy. You can determine both the total expense that will hit the books during the next year and the exact timing of the outgoing cash flows. But then you must face the bigger challenge: figuring out where the money is going to come from. If you are in start-up mode—relying mainly on your initial equity investments or loans to fund your operations—you will have to calculate your burn rate, and then determine whether you will be generating sufficient cash from operations to cover your payroll before your capital is used up. If you are already operating, you will have to project an income statement showing anticipated sales and expenses for the year, and you will have to estimate the timing of the cash flows associated with those sales and expenses. By now you should have a pretty good idea on how to get started on all these tasks.

It is wise to be conservative in these projections. When you hire people, you are asking them to tie their livelihoods to your business. If you expect them to work hard and stick around, the expenses involved are not discretionary. To be sure, we don't mean to be discouraging! Nobody builds a growing business alone, so every entrepreneur who seeks growth will inevitably wind up hiring people. And growing businesses always involve some risk. But we do urge you to apply your financial intelligence to the process so that you don't find yourself overextended and unable to meet payroll.

PATHS TO GROWTH

Though every growth-oriented entrepreneur winds up hiring people, not everyone pursues the same path to growth. In fact, there are four generic strategies that can lead to growth, and each involves a somewhat different combination of financial skills.

More of the Same

Many companies grow simply by doing the same thing they always did, only more of it. They never expand beyond one location. They may add people and equipment as their sales expand, and they may move to a larger building—but it's always the same basic business. Most single-location stores and restaurants fit this model; so do many other small companies, such as consulting firms and job-shop manufacturers.

Managing growth, in this model, first involves seeing the opportunity for more sales and then determining how to make them happen. Can your current mode of turning prospective customers into paying ones handle greater volume? Can your operations handle the increased sales? Do you need to hire more salespeople? If you do, you'll need to develop a compensation plan that meets the needs of the sales reps, that your company can afford, and that will ultimately help the business grow profitably. You will need to project sales and then determine the impact that the increased sales, increased compensation, and increased operational activity are likely to have on your profitability and cash.

Branching Out

Then there's the replication strategy: do the same thing in different locations. The most visible practitioners of this strategy are the big fast-food chains. Many of them operate on a franchise model, but some, such as Starbucks, own all their own stores. You don't have to be a giant to grow by this model. Many entrepreneurial companies, for instance, operate a handful of stores, branch offices, or facilities in a given region.

Deciding to open an additional location is much like buying a piece of capital equipment, but on a larger scale. Just as with any capital expenditure, you need to project cash flow over a period of years, estimate all the expenses for the same time period, and do the calculations that will show you whether the new facility is likely to be a good investment. Companies that grow primarily by adding new facilities typically develop detailed formulas that allow them to project anticipated revenue, expenses, and cash flows with a high degree of accuracy. Nobody's perfect, of course; even Starbucks makes the occasional bad bet and has to close an underperforming store. But the more you do it, the better you will get.

Adding New Products and Services

Many, many entrepreneurial companies begin by focusing on one product or service and gradually branch out into other businesses. Zingerman's, for example, began as a delicatessen but now includes a family of related businesses, including a bake shop, mail-order food, a wholesale coffee roaster, and a consulting firm specializing in customer-service training. Our own company, the Business Literacy Institute, began by focusing purely on customized financial training programs for nonfinancial employees, managers, and leaders. Today it offers several different products and services, including one-on-one financial coaching, Money Maps, and webinars—and of course, the *Financial Intelligence* book series.

You can project results from adding a new product or line of business and analyze the results in the same way you analyze a proposed capital expenditure. But keep in mind that you are dealing with more variables. It can be tough to estimate revenues or cash flows from a new business or product line, just because you don't know that part of the market as well as you know your own. Some companies that add to their lines of business do extensive customer research and invest in the new line only if they are reasonably comfortable that sufficient demand will materialize. Others dip their toes into the waters first. They invest only a modest amount, find a few customers, watch the returns carefully, and invest more only if the new line meets their expectations.

Acquisition

Another time-tested strategy for growth is to buy up similar businesses and either run them independently or incorporate them into your own company. Many well-known companies—Cisco Systems is an example—have grown rapidly through this approach. Entrepreneurs often pursue a variation of the acquisition model known as a roll-up, which involves buying many small companies in the same business (dry-cleaning stores, say) in hopes of building market clout and realizing economies of scale.

Any strategy of acquisition involves a wide variety of financial skills. You must be able to assess the financial situation of a potential acquiree during the process known as due diligence. Is the target company profitable? Has it been relying on any accounting tricks to boost its reported profits or to pretty up its balance sheet? Is its operating cash flow healthy, and has management maintained its asset base? How much is the goodwill worth? These, of course, are just a few of the financial questions you and your team will have to ask.

Then there's the matter of valuation. Given what you find in the due diligence process, what is a fair price to pay for the acquired business? We discussed different methods of valuation in chapter 2, but those are really just starting points. You also need to assess how closely the acquired company will fit with your own business and what level of savings you might realize by eliminating duplication. You need to gauge the prospects for the new, larger company that you are creating. Unlike organic growth, acquisition is a quantum leap: suddenly, you will be managing a significantly larger business than you were before. You need to be sure your financial intelligence—or that of your advisers—is up to the task!

Keep in mind that these are *generic* strategies. In reality, growing companies often rely on a mix of different approaches. (For example, they may buy a competitor and turn it into a branch office that replicates the original business of the acquiring company.) But any growing company needs someone at the helm who understands the financial side of both where the company is today and where it hopes to be a year or five years down the road. Financial intelligence is an indispensable ingredient of any growth strategy.

GOING PUBLIC

This book wouldn't be complete without a few words about going public, which means taking the steps necessary to sell stock to public investors.

To be sure, very few companies in the business population ever go public or even dream of going public. The vast majority of entrepreneurial businesses will begin and end their lives as the property of one owner or a small number of investors. Still, the minority of companies that do go public typically get a lot of press because large sums of money are often at stake. The founders of companies that go public can reap enormous rewards. So can anyone—venture capital firms, for instance—who invested in them when they were still private. The newly public company itself is likely to have a relatively large amount of capital at its disposal with which to expand.

Companies that are candidates for an initial public offering (IPO) generally fall into one of two groups. One is very young companies—often not far beyond the start-up stage—that are thought to hold the potential for explosive growth. They have a new technology or a new business concept that captures the fancy of investors, and they typically need large amounts of outside capital to grow. Many biotech firms, for instance, fall into this category. In the second group are companies that are better established and have already shown that they are capable of rapid and steady, if not explosive, growth. Some restaurant and retail chains are in this category.

If you are planning (or even dreaming) of taking your company public someday, you will want to manage it much like a public company from the very beginning. You will want to find accountants and financial advisers—and ultimately, a financial staff—who are experienced in working with companies heading toward an IPO. You will need audited financial statements every year. You will want to make sure that your own finances and the company's finances are always kept wholly separate. (This is good business practice anyway, but it is particularly important in the case of companies that hope to go public.) You will want to be aware of the restrictions and regulations imposed by Sarbanes-Oxley and other relevant laws (see the toolbox at the end of this part). Going public is often alluring, but the cost of running your business so that you *can* go public is likely to be significant.

Whatever path you choose, we hope that we have helped you with one big part of running your company. We hope you now understand exactly what profit is, and why you need both profit and cash in your business. We hope you understand ratios, so that you can see the trends and opportunities for your business. We hope you know something about managing the balance sheet, so that you can make your company as efficient as possible. We hope you have an understanding of capital expenditure analysis, so that you can make good decisions about where to invest the company's money. We hope you have learned something about all the other elements that make up financial intelligence.

If you want practice using these concepts, we urge you to do the exercises in appendix B or to sit down with your own company's financials and analyze what they tell you. We also suggest passing this book along to the people you work with, so that you can all speak the same language—the language of numbers—and so that they, too, can increase their financial intelligence.

As we said in the preface, we know what it is to start and run a company. It involves a lot of hard work. It can keep you up nights. But it's also one of the most interesting and satisfying endeavors a person can undertake. Increasing your financial intelligence makes the job a little bit easier and a lot more rewarding, because you can better understand what is happening and take the steps you need to take to improve your company's performance. We wish you good luck.

Part Eight
TOOLBOX

OPEN-BOOK MANAGEMENT

Our suggestions about sharing financial information reflect our interest in a philosophy known as open-book management (OBM). Many entrepreneurial companies—including Setpoint, Joe's company—are devotees of this approach. For example, several surveys have found that a significant fraction of *Inc.* magazine's annual list of the five hundred fastest-growing private companies practice some form of OBM.

OBM involves sharing the financials with your employees and, of course, helping them learn what the numbers mean. But it isn't just "open the books"; it's also *managing* with open books. As everyone learns the numbers, people begin to take responsibility for making the numbers move in the right direction, in accordance with monthly or quarterly goals that they help set. ECCO, a safety-equipment manufacturer, began practicing OBM in 1993. The first task, according to CEO Ed Zimmer, was to develop regular weekly "flash" income statements that were accurate. The company then began sponsoring weekly meetings attended by a wide variety of employees, including production employees. Individuals had their initials on line items of the income statement and were held accountable by their peers for the results on that line.

OBM at its best creates an environment where employees feel that they are part of the success—and are at risk for the failure—of the business. This is particularly true when OBM is combined with an employee stock ownership plan or some other form of equity participation. But in some cases a profit-sharing program works as well. At Setpoint, for instance, Joe has seen employees with no stock in the company behave like owners because they know the numbers and have a chance to share in the profits through a bonus. Joe likes to call this psychic ownership.

The classic texts in OBM are *The Great Game of Business* by Jack Stack with Bo Burlingham (Doubleday Currency, 1994), and *Open-Book Management* by John Case (HarperCollins, 1996). You can find more up-to-date information simply by googling the phrase *open-book management*.

UNDERSTANDING SARBANES-OXLEY

If you are reading this book, your company probably isn't publicly traded. So right now, at least, you probably don't have to deal with the law known as Sarbanes-Oxley. But in all likelihood you have read about it in the papers or heard about it from your accountant. And although you don't need to follow the law's rules, you should have a general sense of what it entails. As you grow, you'll want to be sure that what you are doing doesn't veer too far from Sarbanes-Oxley's rules. In many cases, too, your investors, bankers, and even customers and employees will want to know that your financial reporting is valid by the law's standards. And, as we said earlier, if you are thinking that at some point you might want to go public, then you certainly should be paying close attention to the law's requirements.

Sarbanes-Oxley—also known as Sarbox or just Sox—was enacted by the U.S. Congress in July 2002 in response to the continuing revelations of financial fraud at the time. It may be the most significant legislation affecting corporate governance, financial disclosure, and public accounting since the original U.S. securities laws were enacted in the 1930s. It is designed to improve the public's confidence in the financial markets by strengthening financial reporting controls and the penalties for noncompliance.

Sarbanes-Oxley's provisions affect nearly everyone involved with finance. It creates the Public Company Accounting Oversight Board. It bans accounting firms from selling both audit and nonaudit services to clients. It requires corporate boards of directors to include at least one director who is a financial expert, and it requires board audit committees to establish procedures whereby employees can confidentially tip off directors to fraudulent accounting. Under Sarbanes-Oxley, a company cannot fire, demote, or harass employees who attempt to report suspected financial fraud.

CEOs and CFOs are greatly affected by this law. These officers must certify their company's quarterly and annual financial statements, attest that they are responsible for disclosure and control procedures, and affirm that the financial statements don't contain misrepresentations. Executives guilty of intentional misrepresentation may face fines and jail time. Also, the law forbids companies from granting or guaranteeing personal loans to executives and directors. (A study by the nonprofit Corporate Library Research Group found that companies lent executives more than $4.5 billion in 2001, often at no or low interest.) And it requires CEOs or CFOs to give back certain bonuses and stock-option profits if their company is forced to restate financial results because of misconduct.

Sarbanes-Oxley requires companies to strengthen their internal controls. They must include an "internal controls report" in their annual report to shareholders, addressing management's responsibility in maintaining adequate controls over financial reporting and stating a conclusion about the effectiveness of the controls. In addition, management must disclose information on material changes in the financial condition or operations of the company on a rapid and current basis.

Sarbanes-Oxley forces public companies to take more responsibility for their financial statements and may lessen the probability of undetected fraud. However, it is very expensive to implement. The average cost for companies is $5 million; for large companies such as General Electric, it may be as much as $30 million.

If your company is private, you may feel insulated from the effects of Sarbanes-Oxley. But this legislation has an impact on any growing business in the United States. For instance, the accounting profession as a whole has become more conservative in its audits because of the law. As you grow and need financing, most banks and other financing sources will require an audit of your books—and some small private companies have seen the cost of their audits triple because of Sarbanes-Oxley.

Sample Financials

The following is a sample set of financials for an imaginary company.

INCOME STATEMENT *(in thousands)*

	Year ended Dec. 31, 2007
Sales	$8,689
Cost of goods sold	6,756
Gross profit	**$1,933**
Selling, general, and admin. (SG&A)	1,061
Depreciation	239
Other income	19
EBIT	**$ 652**
Interest expense	191
Taxes	213
Net profit	**$ 248**

BALANCE SHEET *(in thousands)*

	Dec. 31, 2007	Dec. 31, 2006
Assets		
Cash and cash equivalents	$ 83	$ 72
Accounts receivable	1,312	1,204
Inventory	1,270	1,514
Other current assets and accruals	85	67
Total current assets	2,750	2,857
Property, plant, and equipment	2,230	2,264
Other long-term assets	213	233
Total assets	**$5,193**	**$5,354**
Liabilities		
Accounts payable	$1,022	$1,129
Credit line	100	150
Current portion of long-term debt	52	51
Total current liabilities	1,174	1,330
Long-term debt	1,037	1,158
Other long-term liabilities	525	491
Total liabilities	**$2,736**	**$2,979**
Shareholders' equity		
Common stock, $1 par value (100,000 authorized, 74,000 outstanding in 2007 and 2006)	$ 74	$ 74
Additional paid-in capital	1,110	1,110
Retained earnings	1,273	1,191
Total shareholders' equity	**$2,457**	**$2,375**
Total liabilities and shareholders' equity	**$5,193**	**$5,354**

2007 footnotes:	
Depreciation	*$239*
Number of common shares (thousands)	*74*
Earnings per share	*$3.35*
Dividend per share	*$2.24*

CASH FLOW STATEMENT *(in thousands)*

	Year ended Dec. 31, 2007
Cash from operating activities	
Net profit	$248
Depreciation	239
Accounts receivable	(108)
Inventory	244
Other current assets	(18)
Accounts payable	(107)
Cash from operations	**$498**
Cash from investing activities	
Property, plant, and equipment	($205)
Other long-term assets	20
Cash from investing	**($185)**
Cash from financing activities	
Credit line	($ 50)
Current portion of long-term debt	1
Long-term debt	(121)
Other long-term liabilities	34
Dividends paid	(166)
Cash from financing	**($302)**
Change in cash	11
Cash at beginning	72
Cash at end	**$ 83**

Exercises to Build Your Financial Intelligence

Income Statement Exercise

The following exercises will give you the opportunity to practice what you learned about the income statement.

Our goals with this practice are for you to:

- *Get comfortable reading an income statement.* Half the battle is simply learning to find the right data, so we'll ask you to find the numbers that you'll need to do some analysis.

- *Begin to analyze the results.* By looking at the trends and doing a few simple percentage calculations, you'll start to see a layer of meaning behind the numbers.

- *Understand the meaning of the numbers.* You will answer a few questions about the numbers that will help you understand their significance.

EXERCISE DESCRIPTION

There are two income statements, one for Under Armour and one for eBay, in appendix C. You can practice with one or both. We've included these two companies because one is a manufacturer and one is a service company. Of course, there are many other types of organizations (retail, banking, nonprofit, and so on), but two will give you a good start.

A few cautions: because one company is in manufacturing and one is a service business, the income statements contain some different line items. Even common line items may be labeled differently. Remember, too, that these two companies are just samples—other manufacturers' and service companies' statements will have slightly different line items and labels. But once you familiarize yourself with the key lines, you'll be able to work your way through most financial statements.

Follow the instructions here, and you'll be building your financial intelligence.

INSTRUCTIONS

1. Choose which company's financial information you want to work with, and then find the correct table to fill in. The tables are different because the two companies' income statements have different line items. Use the tables to enter your numbers or as a guide to write your answers on a separate piece of paper or in a spreadsheet.

2. Try your hand at the calculations and questions. You'll see the calculation to do (either a "percent of" or a "percent change" calculation), a column for the data, and a column for the results. Pay close attention to the year you are working on, and be sure your data and results match the correct year. That will help you later when you are looking at trends. The tables and questions are labeled for Under Armour and for eBay. Doing the calculations and answering the questions will give you an opportunity to think about what the numbers you just wrote down mean.

3. Step back and be proud of your work!

4. Take a look at the answers and see how you did. (Yes, the answers are right here. We don't want you to have to flip back and forth, and it is OK if you peek. The whole point is to learn. This is not a test!)

CALCULATIONS

Really do try these—you'll be surprised at how easy they are and how much more information you'll have about the company once you do them.

Under Armour, Inc. and Subsidiaries

Percent of:

	2006 Data	2006 Result	2005 Data	2005 Result	2004 Data	2004 Result
Gross profit as a percent of net revenues						
Selling, general, and administrative expenses as a percent of net revenues						
Income from operations as a percent of net revenues						

Percent Change:

	2005 to 2006 Data	2005 to 2006 Result	2004 to 2005 Data	2004 to 2005 Result
Percent change in net revenues				
Percent change in income from operations				

eBay Inc.

Percent of:

	2006 Data	2006 Result	2005 Data	2005 Result	2004 Data	2004 Result
Gross profit as a percent of net revenues						
Sales and marketing as a percent of net revenues						
General and administrative as a percent of net revenues						
Income from operations as a percent of net revenues						

Percent Change:

	2005 to 2006 Data	2005 to 2006 Result	2004 to 2005 Data	2004 to 2005 Result
Percent change in net revenues				
Percent change in income from operations				

QUESTIONS

Now let's try answering a few questions. You can answer them for one or both companies:

1. What trends do you see by looking at the income statement itself, the raw numbers? What are they telling you?

   Under Armour:

   _____

   _____

   _____

eBay:

_____

_____

_____

2. Look at your percent of and percent change results. What are they telling you?

   Under Armour:

   _____

   _____

   _____

   eBay:

   _____

   _____

   _____

CALCULATION RESULTS

Under Armour, Inc. and Subsidiaries

Percent of:

	2006 Data	2006 Result	2005 Data	2005 Result	2004 Data	2004 Result
Gross profit as a percent of net revenues	215,600 430,689	50.1%	135,850 281,053	48.3%	95,433 205,181	46.5%
Selling, general, and administrative expenses as a percent of net revenues	158,323 430,689	36.8%	99,961 281,053	35.6%	70,053 205,181	34.1%
Income from operations as a percent of net revenues	57,277 430,689	13.3%	35,889 281,053	12.8%	25,380 205,181	12.4%

Percent Change:

	2005 to 2006 Data	2005 to 2006 Result	2004 to 2005 Data	2004 to 2005 Result
Percent change in net revenues	$\dfrac{430,689 - 281,053}{281,053}$	53.2%	$\dfrac{281,053 - 205,181}{205,181}$	37.0%
Percent change in income from operations	$\dfrac{57,277 - 35,889}{35,889}$	59.6%	$\dfrac{35,889 - 25,380}{25,380}$	41.4%

eBay Inc.

Percent of:

	2006 Data	2006 Result	2005 Data	2005 Result	2004 Data	2004 Result
Gross profit as a percent of net revenues	$\dfrac{4,712,949}{5,969,741}$	79.06%	$\dfrac{3,734,297}{4,552,401}$	82.0%	$\dfrac{2,656,894}{3,271,309}$	81.2%
Sales and marketing as a percent of net revenues	$\dfrac{1,619,857}{5,969,741}$	27.1%	$\dfrac{1,185,929}{4,552,401}$	26.1%	$\dfrac{815,464}{3,271,309}$	24.9%
General and administrative as a percent of net revenues	$\dfrac{978,363}{5,969,741}$	16.4%	$\dfrac{649,529}{4,552,401}$	14.3%	$\dfrac{475,614}{3,271,309}$	14.5%
Income from operations as a percent of net revenues	$\dfrac{1,422,956}{5,969,741}$	23.8%	$\dfrac{1,441,707}{4,552,401}$	31.7%	$\dfrac{1,059,242}{3,271,309}$	32.4%

Percent Change:

	2005 to 2006 Data	2005 to 2006 Result	2004 to 2005 Data	2004 to 2005 Result
Percent change in net revenues	$\dfrac{5,969,741 - 4,552,401}{4,552,401}$	31.1%	$\dfrac{4,552,401 - 3,271,309}{3,271,309}$	39.2%
Percent change in income from operations	$\dfrac{1,422,956 - 1,441,707}{1,441,707}$	(1.3%)	$\dfrac{1,441,707 - 1,059,242}{1,059,242}$	36.1%

ANSWERS TO THE QUESTIONS

Here are just a few thoughts in response to each of the questions we asked you to consider. There is certainly plenty of data to look at, with various possible conclusions, so there is no one right answer. These answers are just to give you a flavor of what you might look at as you study the results.

1. What trends do you see in the raw numbers? What are they telling you?

   Under Armour: The trend is great—just what an investor would hope to see. Gross margin improved from 46.5 percent in 2004 to 50.1 percent in 2006. Operating margins improved as well. The only area of concern is the increasing SG&A as a percent of revenue: it rose from 34.1 percent in 2004 to 38.6 percent in 2006. We would like to see this ratio improving as the company grows, not getting worse.

   eBay: EBay appears to be facing a challenge. All its margins are decreasing while its costs relative to revenue are increasing. EBay needs to reverse this trend. This is particularly true for G&A: from 2005 to 2006, G&A as a percent of revenue rose from 14.3 percent to 16.4 percent.

2. Look at your percent of and percent change results. What are they telling you?

   Under Armour: Under Armour is growing fast. Investors like to see more growth in operating profit than in revenue—exactly what is happening here.

   eBay: EBay is interesting. Revenue is growing rapidly, but margin actually decreased from 2005 to 2006. This is a concern for eBay. The declining margin could be due to competition in the marketplace or to significant increases in costs.

INTERESTING THINGS TO NOTE

- Remember that many terms mean the same thing and that sometimes the same company will use different terms to indicate the same thing. Here, both Under Armour and eBay use the terms *gross profit* and *net income* for the various forms of profit. Keep an eye out for those differences, and remember it is all one form or another of profit.

- Note that eBay shows more detail in the operating expenses section, with line items for sales and marketing, product development, and general and administrative categories. Under Armour just includes the line item selling, general, and administrative expenses. Companies have discretion about the level of detail they provide.

- Although this might seem insignificant, take a look at how the statements are laid out. Under Armour indents the total lines, and eBay does not. Each time you read a financial statement, one of the first things you should do is figure out the layout. Doing so makes it much easier to find what you are looking for.

- Both statements are for the year ended December 31. Remember, companies can use any year-end they want to, although they must be consistent and must disclose any change in year-end. Both statements are also "in thousands," except for per-share amounts. That means that the "true" numbers have three additional zeros, except for the last sections of each statement.

- Although it is typical to call net profit the "bottom line," you can see that the real bottom line in both these statements is per-share data— that is, data based on the number of common shares outstanding. Be careful: sometimes those line item names will be very close to what you might expect for net profit. Check to be sure they are not per-share data.

Balance Sheet Exercise

The balance sheet is a little tougher than the income statement, but remember that this is the statement that outsiders look at first. If you really understand it, you might start doing that, too.

Once again, our goals for you are:

- *To get comfortable reading the balance sheet.* You'll get more practice finding certain numbers.

- *To begin to analyze the results.* You'll do just a little analysis here. There will be more later, in the ratios exercise.

- *To understand the numbers you are finding.* The questions will help you do just that.

EXERCISE DESCRIPTION

The balance sheets for Under Armour and eBay are found in appendix C. Do one or both. The general exercise is the same as in the income statement exercise: use the appropriate table and then analyze the results.

INSTRUCTIONS

1. Based on the financial statement of your choice, find the appropriate table.

2. Try your hand at the calculations and questions. You'll see the formula, a column for the data, and a column for the result, just as with the income statement calculations. There are only a few calculations to do with the balance sheet for now. You'll do more when we get to ratios. Doing the calculations and answering the questions will give you an opportunity to think about what the numbers mean.

3. Step back and be proud of your work!

4. Take a look at the answers and see how you did.

CALCULATIONS

Let's do the calculations. For the balance sheet calculations, the names of the categories are the same, so do these calculations for both companies (of course, only if you want to practice).

Under Armour, Inc. and Subsidiaries

	2005 to 2006 Data	2005 to 2006 Result
Percent change in total assets		
Percent change in total liabilities		

eBay Inc.

	2005 to 2006 Data	2005 to 2006 Result
Percent change in total assets (shown but not labeled)		
Percent change in total liabilities		

QUESTIONS

Now let's try answering a few questions:

1. What trends do you see in the raw numbers? What are they telling you?

    Under Armour:

    _____

    _____

    _____

    eBay:

    _____

    _____

    _____

2. Look at your percent change results. What are they telling you?

    Under Armour:

    _____

    _____

    _____

    eBay:

    _____

    _____

    _____

CALCULATION RESULTS

Under Armour, Inc. and Subsidiaries

	2005 to 2006 Data	2005 to 2006 Result
Percent change in total assets	$\dfrac{289,368 - 203,687}{203,687}$	42.1%
Percent change in total liabilities	$\dfrac{74,980 - 52,857}{52,857}$	41.9%

eBay Inc.

	2005 to 2006 Data	2005 to 2006 Result
Percent change in total assets (shown but not labeled)	$\dfrac{13,494,011 - 11,788,986}{11,788,986}$	14.5%
Percent change in total liabilities	$\dfrac{2,589,379 - 1,741,005}{1,741,005}$	48.7%

ANSWERS TO THE QUESTIONS

As in the income statement exercise, here are just a few thoughts in response to each of the questions we asked you to consider about the balance sheet results.

1.   What trends do you see in the raw numbers? What are they telling you?

> *Under Armour:* Under Armour looks great. Its cash is strong, and it is growing a lot of equity on its balance sheet. It is also paying down its long-term debt. This company has very little debt relative to its equity.

> *eBay:* EBay looks strong on the balance sheet. There is a sharp increase in current liabilities, but the company has lots of cash. EBay does not have any long-term debt. This is very conservative but may be warranted because of the company's declining margins.

2.   Look at your percent change results. What are they telling you?

> *Under Armour:* Under Armour is consistent. Its asset and liability growth are close together. It appears to be a stable company in the years presented here.

> *eBay:* EBay's liabilities are growing faster than its assets. It has plenty of cash, so that should not be a major concern in the short term. If the trend continues, it should be watched closely.

INTERESTING THINGS TO NOTE

• The asset line items are slightly different in the two statements, based at least in part on their different businesses. For example, Under Armour has inventory and eBay doesn't, as you would expect. Only eBay has goodwill, which tells us that it has acquired at least one company. In accounts receivable, Under Armour gives us the details for its allowance for doubtful accounts; eBay simply lists its accounts receivable number as net, without providing the detail (although we bet you'd be able to find it in the footnotes). As we've discussed, companies have latitude in how they present their numbers, as long as they are consistent and disclose any changes.

• The liability line items are different, again based on the difference in the businesses. For example, eBay has lines that relate to its business, such as funds payable, amounts due to customers, deferred revenue, and customer advances. These are liabilities related to eBay's business model. Under Armour has more typical liability line items.

• Under Armour and eBay use different names for the stockholders' equity section. Under Armour's title is "Stockholders' equity and comprehensive loss," while eBay is simply "Stockholders' equity." Under Armour's title is descriptive of what is included in that section.

• Neither company provides all the totals that would be helpful in reading the statements. For example, eBay includes but does not label total assets or the total of liabilities and stockholders' equity. Often it is difficult to see the dividing line between liabilities and stockholders' equity, just because the sections run together. One way of ensuring you have all your numbers correct: add up what you think are all the liabilities, and then add that to the stockholders' equity. If that total is the same as total assets, you have the right answer.

Cash Flow Statement Exercise

OK, let's practice the cash flow statement. Here we'll just look at the numbers and trends but not do any calculations (whew—enough already with the calculator!).

To review, our goals for you are:

- *To get comfortable reading the cash flow statement.*

- *To understand the numbers you find.*

- *To be able to identify where the cash is coming from and where it is going.*

EXERCISE DESCRIPTION

Once again, pick Under Armour, eBay, or both, and use the tables. Then answer the questions that follow.

INSTRUCTIONS

1. Using the financial statement of your choice, find the line items indicated in the table in the appropriate cash flow statement for 2006, 2005, and 2004.

2. After you've finished, answer the questions. They will help you think about the numbers you just found.

3. Step back and be proud of your work!

4. Take a look at the answers and see how you did.

Under Armour, Inc. and Subsidiaries: Consolidated Statements of Cash Flows, in thousands

Years ended December 31

	2006	2005	2004
Net cash provided by (used in) operating activities			
Net cash used in investing activities			
Net cash provided by financing activities			
Net increase in cash and cash equivalents			
Cash and cash equivalents, beginning of year			
Cash and cash equivalents, end of year			

eBay Inc.: Consolidated Statement of Cash Flows, in thousands

Years ended December 31

	2006	2005	2004
Net cash provided by operating activities			
Net cash (used in) provided by investing activities			
Net cash provided by (used in) financing activities			
Net increase (decrease) in cash and cash equivalents			
Cash and cash equivalents at beginning of period			
Cash and cash equivalents at end of period			

QUESTIONS

Now for a few thought-provoking questions:

1. Where is the cash coming from? Is it from operations (the business of the company), from investing, or from financing? What might that mean?

    Under Armour:

    _____

    _____

    _____

    eBay:

    _____

    _____

    _____

2. What are the trends in the three categories of cash?

    Under Armour:

    _____

    _____

    _____

    eBay:

    _____

    _____

    _____

CASH FLOW DATA RESULTS

Under Armour, Inc. and Subsidiaries: Consolidated Statements of Cash Flows, in thousands

Year ended December 31

	2006	2005	2004
Net cash provided by (used in) operating activities	10,701	15,795	(8,851)
Net cash used in investing activities	(15,115)	(10,833)	(8,683)
Net cash provided by financing activities	12,579	56,989	18,004
Net increase in cash and cash equivalents	7,678	61,892	418
Cash and cash equivalents, beginning of year	62,977	1,085	667
Cash and cash equivalents, end of year	70,655	62,977	1,085

eBay Inc.: Consolidated Statement of Cash Flows, in thousands

Year ended December 31

	2006	2005	2004
Net cash provided by operating activities	2,247,791	2,009,891	1,285,315
Net cash (used in) provided by investing activities	228,853	(2,452,731)	(2,013,220)
Net cash provided by (used in) financing activities	(1,260,687)	471,606	647,669
Net increase (decrease) in cash and cash equivalents	1,349,212	(16,465)	(51,468)
Cash and cash equivalents at beginning of period	1,313,580	1,330,045	1,381,513
Cash and cash equivalents at end of period	2,662,792	1,313,580	1,330,045

ANSWERS TO THE QUESTIONS

Here are our thoughts in response to each of the questions we asked you to consider.

1. Where is the cash coming from? Is it from operations (the business of the company), from investing, or from financing? What might that mean?

   Under Armour: For Under Armour, cash is coming from investors through stock sales in 2004 and from operations in 2005 and 2006. The company seems to have turned the corner in terms of operating cash flow.

   eBay: EBay has very strong operating cash flow. This somewhat mitigates the concern about its margins. It will be interesting to see how eBay's cash flow is in future years. This strong operating cash flow is a good sign for the business.

2. What are the trends in the three categories of cash?

   Under Armour: Under Armour is growing but was still getting positive operating cash flow in 2005 and 2006. It is investing heavily, and it was financing some of this investment through sizable equity investments in 2005. Overall, primary financing for the business is coming from operations and equity financing.

   eBay: EBay is generating great cash from operations and was using the cash for investments in 2004 and 2005. In 2006 the company stopped investing and bought back a large portion of stock. This is a sign that the company believes the stock price is relatively low and that the cash generation from operations is going to continue. EBay is a strong company in terms of cash flow.

INTERESTING THINGS TO NOTE

• Remember that every company uses its own terminology. It just happens that these two companies use the same terms for the main categories of cash flow (cash flows from operating activities, cash flows from investing activities, and cash flows from financing activities). However, take a look at the totals for each category. You will get a flavor of both the differences and the difficulties in reading the cash flow statement. For the first category, cash flows from operating activities, Under Armour's total says, "Net cash provided by (used in) operating activities." This means that in one or more years cash was positive from operations (no parentheses), and in the other years cash was negative from operations (parentheses). Look at the numbers, and you'll see that in 2006 and 2005 cash was positive, but in 2004 it was negative. So 2004 is the year that net cash was "(used in)" operations. The line item label should always indicate what the parentheses mean.

• Remember that the cash flow statement is the most difficult to read. But now that we have real numbers, you can see how it works in action. Look at accounts receivable for Under Armour. On the balance sheet, you can see that accounts receivable went up from 2005 to 2006 by $20,828. When accounts receivable increases, other things being equal, cash goes down. Now look at the cash flow statement. The accounts receivable line in the "cash flows from operating activities" section shows a negative total of $20,828 (we know it is negative because it is in parentheses). That is the same amount that accounts receivable changed from one year to the next on the balance sheet.

Ratios Exercise

Now we get to put it all together and calculate some ratios for our two sample companies, Under Armour and eBay. Remember what we said when we introduced ratios: that ratios give us more information than the raw numbers alone. So let's see what our ratios can tell us.

Once again, our goals for you are as follows:

- *To find the numbers required to calculate the ratios.*

- *To get comfortable using the ratio formulas.*

- *To get you thinking about what the ratios mean.*

EXERCISE DESCRIPTION

Depending on which ratio you'll be calculating, you'll be using one or more of Under Armour's or eBay's financial statements. Again, you can calculate the ratios for one or both companies. Here it might be really interesting to do both. Some of the differences between a manufacturing company and a service company will reveal themselves in ratio results.

You won't be calculating all the ratios you learned in part 5, just enough to get a good feel for how ratios work and what they might tell you. Also, you won't calculate exactly the same ratios for Under Armour as you will for eBay. For example, eBay doesn't have inventory, so you can't calculate days in inventory or inventory turnover.

You may have noticed in the previous practices that the language in the tables matched the financial statements exactly. That was to minimize confusion. In real life, however, everyone will be using different terminology. So this time our formulas are generic: we use just one word for profit, sales, and so on, and you will need to find the appropriate line item, even if it doesn't match exactly. With as much reading as you've been doing, we are confident you'll master this challenge.

Your next step, after you finish this book, is to get the financials for your own company and calculate all the ratios that make sense for your type of organization. That should tell you a lot about your company—information you'll be able to use in running the business.

INSTRUCTIONS

1. Calculate the ratios indicated. We've listed the name of the ratio and the formula to use. Then there are columns for the longhand calculation and the result. Use these tables, a separate piece of paper, or a spreadsheet.

2. After you've finished, answer the questions that follow the table. They will help you look at your results with a critical eye.

3. Step back and be proud of your work!

4. Take a look at the answers in the next set of tables and see how you did.

Under Armour, Inc. and Subsidiaries: Ratio Table

	Formula	2006 Data	2006 Result	2005 Data	2005 Result
Profitability ratios					
Gross profit margin percentage	Gross profit / Revenue				
Operating profit margin percentage	Operating profit / Revenue				
Return on assets	Net profit / Total assets				
Return on equity	Net profit / Shareholders' equity				
Leverage ratio					
Debt-to-equity	Total liabilities / Shareholders' equity				
Liquidity ratio					
Current ratio	Current assets / Current liabilities				

(*continued*)

	Formula	2006 Data	2006 Result	2005 Data	2005 Result
Efficiency ratios					
Inventory days (DII)	$\dfrac{\text{Average inventory}}{\text{COGS/day}}$				Don't have 2004 data, so can't calculate.
Inventory turns	$\dfrac{360}{\text{DII}}$				Don't have DII, so can't calculate.
Days sales outstanding	$\dfrac{\text{Ending A/R}}{\text{Revenue/day}}$				
PPE turnover	$\dfrac{\text{Revenue}}{\text{PPE}}$				
Total asset turnover	$\dfrac{\text{Revenue}}{\text{Total assets}}$				

eBay Inc.: Ratio Table

	Formula	2006 Data	2006 Result	2005 Data	2005 Result
Profitability ratios					
Gross profit margin percentage	$\dfrac{\text{Gross profit}}{\text{Revenue}}$				
Operating profit margin percentage	$\dfrac{\text{Operating profit}}{\text{Revenue}}$				
Net profit margin percentage	$\dfrac{\text{Net profit}}{\text{Revenue}}$				
Return on assets	$\dfrac{\text{Net profit}}{\text{Total assets}}$				

	Formula	2006 Data	2006 Result	2005 Data	2005 Result
Return on equity	Net profit / Shareholders' equity				
Leverage ratio					
Debt-to-equity	Total liabilities / Shareholders' equity				
Liquidity ratio					
Current ratio	Current assets / Current liabilities				
Efficiency ratios					
Days sales outstanding	Ending A/R / Revenue/day				
PPE turnover	Revenue / PPE				
Total asset turnover	Revenue / Total assets				

QUESTIONS

Now let's consider the results.

1. What do the ratio results tell you that the raw numbers didn't? For example, what do the profitability ratios tell you that the raw numbers didn't?

    Under Armour:

    _____

    _____

    _____

eBay:

_____

_____

_____

2. What do you see in the leverage and liquidity ratio results?

Under Armour:

_____

_____

_____

eBay:

_____

_____

_____

3. What are the trends in the efficiency ratios?

Under Armour:

_____

_____

_____

eBay:

_____

_____

_____

CALCULATION RESULTS

Now let's see how you did.

Under Armour, Inc. and Subsidiaries: Ratio Results

	Formula	2006 Data	2006 Result	2005 Data	2005 Result
Profitability ratios					
Gross profit margin percentage	Gross profit / Revenue	215,600 430,689	50.1%	135,850 281,053	48.3%
Operating profit margin percentage	Operating profit / Revenue	57,277 430,689	13.3%	35,899 281,053	12.8%
Return on assets	Net profit / Total assets	38,979 289,368	13.5%	19,719 203,687	9.7%
Return on equity	Net profit / Shareholders' equity	38,979 214,388	18.2%	19,719 150,830	13.1%
Leverage ratio					
Debt-to-equity	Total liabilities / Shareholders' equity	74,980 214,388	.35	52,857 150,830	.35
Liquidity ratio					
Current ratio	Current assets / Current liabilities	244,952 71,563	3.42	181,790 47,672	3.81
Efficiency ratios					
Inventory days (DII)	Average inventory / COGS/day	(81,031+ 53,607)/2 215,089/ 360	112.67 days	Don't have 2004 data, so can't calculate.	
Inventory turns	360 / DII	360 112.67	3.20	Don't have DII, so can't calculate.	

(*continued*)

	Formula	2006 Data	2006 Result	2005 Data	2005 Result
Efficiency ratios *continued*					
Days sales outstanding	Ending A/R / Revenue/day	71,867 / 430,689/ 360	60.1 days	53,132 / 281,053/ 360	68.1 days
PPE turnover	Revenue / PPE	430,689 / 29,923	14.39	281,053 / 20,865	13.47
Total asset turnover	Revenue / Total assets	430,689 / 289,368	1.49	281,053 / 203,687	1.38

eBay Inc.: Ratio Results

	Formula	2006 Data	2006 Result	2005 Data	2005 Result
Profitability ratios					
Gross profit margin percentage	Gross profit / Revenue	4,712,949 / 5,969,741	79.0%	3,734,297 / 4,552,401	82.0%
Operating profit margin percentage	Operating profit / Revenue	1,422,956 / 5,969,741	23.8%	1,441,707 / 4,552,401	31.7%
Net profit margin percentage	Net profit / Revenue	1,125,639 / 5,969,741	18.9%	1,082,043 / 4,552,401	23.8%
Return on assets	Net profit / Total assets	1,125,639 / 13,494,011	8.3%	1,082,043 / 11,788,986	9.2%
Return on equity	Net profit / Shareholders' equity	1,125,639 / 10,904,632	10.3%	1,082,043 / 10,047,981	10.8%
Leverage ratio					
Debt-to-equity	Total liabilities / Shareholders' equity	2,589,379 / 10,904,632	.24	1,741,005 / 10,047,981	.17

	Formula	2006 Data	2006 Result	2005 Data	2005 Result
Liquidity ratio					
Current ratio	Current assets / Current liabilities	4,970,586 / 2,518,395	1.97	3,183,237 / 1,484,935	2.14
Efficiency ratios					
Days sales outstanding	Ending A/R / Revenue/day	393,195 / 5,969,741/ 360	23.7 days	322,788 / 4,552,401/ 360	25.5 days
PPE turnover	Revenue / PPE	5,969,741 / 998,196	5.98	4,552,401 / 801,602	5.68
Total asset turnover	Revenue / Total assets	5,969,741 / 13,494,011	.44	4,552,401 / 11,788,986	.39

ANSWERS TO THE QUESTIONS

Interpreting these ratios accurately would require us to know a lot about the companies in question. We don't work for Under Armour or eBay, and we aren't analysts studying the companies over time. The following responses, therefore, are just a few thoughts on the little information that we do have.

1. What do the ratio results tell you that the raw numbers didn't? For example, what do the profitability ratios tell you that the raw numbers didn't?

   Under Armour: Under Armour is improving its margins and getting an improving return on its assets and equity. The company is holding its debt constant as it grows. It is apparently improving its asset management.

   eBay: While eBay is growing rapidly, it is losing ground in terms of profitability. It has slightly lower returns on assets and equity from 2005 to 2006. This is a trend that investors would want to keep an eye on for 2007.

2. What do you see in the leverage and liquidity ratio results?

   Under Armour: Under Armour has plenty of working capital and a very high current ratio. It is a low-debt business—only $0.35 of debt for every dollar of equity. This company may be able to improve its return for its shareholders by increasing its use of debt to finance the business.

   eBay: EBay is a business that is financed mostly by equity. This is typical for an Internet-based technology company. Its debt-to-equity ratio increased in 2006 mostly because of a significant stock buyback. The company had plenty of cash and a high current ratio that actually increased from 2.14 in 2005 to 2.30 in 2006.

3. What are the trends in the efficiency ratios?

   Under Armour: Under Armour is getting more efficient. Its days sales outstanding (DSO) improved, and its total asset turnover improved significantly, from 1.38 to 1.49. This is a sign of a maturing and more efficient business.

eBay: EBay is getting more efficient at asset management. Its DSO improved, and its total asset turnover improved from .39 in 2005 to .44 in 2006. One way to offset the effect of lower margins is to improve asset efficiency. Unfortunately, the improvement in asset management was not enough to overcome the lower margin in 2006; that's why return on assets decreased from 9.2 percent in 2005 to 8.3 percent in 2006.

Under Armour and eBay Financial Statements

Under Armour, Inc. and Subsidiaries
Consolidated Statements of Income
(in thousands, except per share amounts)

	Year Ended December 31,		
	2006	2005	2004
Net revenues	$430,689	$281,053	$205,181
Cost of goods sold	215,089	145,203	109,748
Gross profit	215,600	135,850	95,433
Operating expenses			
Selling, general and administrative expenses	158,323	99,961	70,053
Income from operations	57,277	35,889	25,380
Other income (expense), net	1,810	(2,915)	(1,284)
Income before income taxes	59,087	32,974	24,096
Provision for income taxes	20,108	13,255	7,774
Net income	38,979	19,719	16,322
Accretion of and cumulative preferred dividends on Series A Preferred Stock	—	5,307	1,994
Net income available to common stockholders	$ 38,979	$ 14,412	$ 14,328
Net income available per common share			
Basic	$ 0.83	$ 0.39	$ 0.41
Diluted	$ 0.79	$ 0.36	$ 0.39
Weighted average common shares outstanding			
Basic	46,983	37,199	35,124
Diluted	49,587	39,686	36,774

See accompanying notes.

Under Armour, Inc. and Subsidiaries
Consolidated Balance Sheets
(in thousands, except share data)

	December 31,	
	2006	2005
Assets		
Current Assets		
Cash and cash equivalents	$ 70,655	$ 62,977
Accounts receivable, net of allowance for doubtful accounts of $884 and $521 as of December 31, 2006 and 2005, respectively	71,867	53,132
Inventories	81,031	53,607
Income taxes receivable	4,310	—
Prepaid expenses and other current assets	8,944	5,252
Deferred income taxes	8,145	6,822
Total current assets	244,952	181,790
Property and equipment, net	29,923	20,865
Intangible asset, net	7,875	—
Deferred income taxes	5,180	—
Other non-current assets	1,438	1,032
Total assets	$289,368	$203,687
Liabilities and Stockholders' Equity		
Current liabilities		
Accounts payable	$ 42,718	$ 31,699
Accrued expenses	25,403	11,449
Income taxes payable	—	716
Current maturities of long term debt	2,648	1,967
Current maturities of capital lease obligations	794	1,841
Total current liabilities	71,563	47,672
Long term debt, net of current maturities	1,893	2,868
Capital lease obligations, net of current maturities	922	1,715
Deferred income taxes	—	330
Other long term liabilities	602	272
Total liabilities	74,980	52,857
Commitments and contingencies (see Note 8)		
Stockholders' equity and comprehensive loss		
Class A Common Stock, $.0003 1/3 par value; 100,000,000 shares authorized as of December 31, 2006 and 2005, 34,555,907 shares issued and outstanding as of December 31, 2006; 31,223,351 shares issued and outstanding as of December 31, 2005	12	10
Class B Convertible Common Stock, $.0003 1/3 par value; 16,200,000 shares authorized as of December 31, 2006 and 2005, 13,250,000 shares issued and outstanding as of December 31, 2006; 15,200,000 shares issued and outstanding as of December 31, 2005	4	5
Additional paid-in capital	148,562	124,803
Retained earnings	66,376	28,067
Unearned compensation	(463)	(1,889)
Notes receivable from stockholders	—	(163)
Accumulated other comprehensive loss	(103)	(3)
Total stockholders' equity	214,388	150,830
Total liabilities and stockholders' equity	$289,368	$203,687

See accompanying notes.

Under Armour, Inc. and Subsidiaries
Consolidated Statements of Cash Flows
(in thousands)

	Year Ended December 31,		
	2006	2005	2004
Cash flows from operating activities			
Net income	$ 38,979	$ 19,719	$ 16,322
Adjustments to reconcile net income to net cash provided by (used in) operating activities			
Depreciation and amortization	9,824	6,546	3,174
Unrealized foreign exchange rate loss	161	—	—
Loss on disposal of fixed assets	115	58	591
Stock-based compensation	1,982	1,177	—
Deferred income taxes	(6,721)	(331)	(3,341)
Changes in reserves for doubtful accounts, returns, discounts and inventories	3,832	3,150	4,610
Changes in operating assets and liabilities:			
Accounts receivable	(20,828)	(17,552)	(18,811)
Inventories	(26,504)	(5,669)	(27,195)
Prepaid expenses and other current assets	(3,674)	(2,723)	(615)
Other non-current assets	(323)	(157)	(69)
Accounts payable	8,203	11,074	9,747
Accrued expenses and other liabilities	10,681	1,990	5,504
Income taxes payable and receivable	(5,026)	(1,487)	(1,232)
Net cash provided by (used in) operating activities	10,701	15,795	(8,851)
Cash flows from investing activities			
Purchase of property and equipment	(15,115)	(10,887)	(8,724)
Proceeds from sale of property and equipment	—	54	41
Purchases of short-term investments	(89,650)	—	—
Proceeds from sales of short-term investments)	89,650	—	—
Net cash used in investing activities	(15,115)	(10,833)	(8,683)
Cash flows from financing activities			
Proceeds from long-term debt	2,119	3,944	450
Payments on long-term debt	(2,413)	(26,711)	(524)
Payments on capital lease obligations	(1,840)	(2,330)	(1,424)
Net (payments) proceeds from revolving credit facility	—	(13,748)	19,457
Payments of common stock dividends	—	(5,000)	—
Excess tax benefits from stock-based compensation arrangements	11,260	—	—
Proceeds from exercise of stock options and other stock issuances	3,544	990	78
Payments of debt financing costs	(260)	(1,061)	(50)
Payments received on notes from stockholders	169	229	17
Proceeds from sale of Class A Common Stock	—	123,500	—

continued

Under Armour, Inc. and Subsidiaries
Consolidated Statements of Cash Flows
(in thousands) *continued*

	Year Ended December 31,		
	2006	2005	2004
Payments of stock issue costs	—	(10,824)	—
Redemption of Series A Preferred Stock	—	(12,000)	—
Net cash provided by financing activities	12,579	56,989	18,004
Effect of exchange rate changes on cash and cash equivalents	(487)	(59)	(52)
Net increase in cash and cash equivalents	7,678	61,892	418
Cash and cash equivalents			
Beginning of year	62,977	1,085	667
End of year	$70,655	$62,977	$ 1,085
Non-cash financing and investing activities			
Fair market value of shares withheld in consideration of employee tax obligations relative to stock-based compensation	$ 734	$ —	$ —
Accretion of and cumulative preferred dividends on Series A Preferred Stock	—	5,307	1,994
Purchase of equipment through debt obligations	2,700	2,103	5,156
Issuance of warrants in partial consideration for intangible asset	8,500	—	—
Settlement of outstanding accounts receivable with property and equipment	350	—	—
Reversal of unearned compensation and additional paid in capital due to adoption of SFAS 123R	715	—	—
Exercise of stock-based compensation arrangements through stockholders' notes receivable	—	262	—
Transfer of revolving credit facility to term debt		25,000	—
Unpaid declared common stock dividends	—	—	5,000
Other supplemental information			
Cash paid for income taxes	20,522	15,204	9,775
Cash paid for interest	531	2,866	1,281

See accompanying notes.

eBay Inc.
CONSOLIDATED STATEMENT OF INCOME

	Year Ended December 31,		
	2004	**2005**	**2006**
	(In thousands, except per share amounts)		
Net revenues	$3,271,309	$4,552,401	$5,969,741
Cost of net revenues	614,415	818,104	1,256,792
Gross profit	2,656,894	3,734,297	4,712,949
Operating expenses:			
Sales and marketing	815,464	1,185,929	1,619,857
Product development	240,647	328,191	494,695
General and administrative	475,614	649,529	978,363
Amortization of acquired intangible assets	65,927	128,941	197,078
Total operating expenses	1,597,652	2,292,590	3,289,993
Income from operations	1,059,242	1,441,707	1,422,956
Interest and other income, net	77,867	111,148	130,021
Interest expense	(8,879)	(3,478)	(5,916)
Income before income taxes and minority interests	1,128,230	1,549,377	1,547,061
Provision for income taxes	(343,885)	(467,285)	(421,418)
Minority interests	(6,122)	(49)	(4)
Net income	$ 778,223	$ 1,082,043	$ 1,125,639
Net income per share:			
Basic	$ 0.59	$ 0.79	$ 0.80
Diluted	$ 0.57	$ 0.78	$ 0.79
Weighted average shares:			
Basic	1,319,458	1,361,708	1,399,251
Diluted	1,367,720	1,393,875	1,425,472

The accompanying notes are an integral part of these consolidated financial statements.

eBay Inc.
CONSOLIDATED BALANCE SHEET

	December 31,	
	2005	**2006**
	(In thousands, except par value amounts)	
ASSETS		
Current Assets:		
Cash and cash equivalents	$ 1,313,580	$ 2,662,792
Short-term investments	774,650	542,103
Accounts receivable, net	322,788	393,195
Funds receivable from customers	255,282	399,297
Restricted cash	29,702	12,738
Other current assets	487,235	960,461
Total current assets	3,183,237	4,970,586
Long-term investments	825,667	277,853
Property and equipment, net	801,602	998,196
Goodwill	6,120,079	6,544,278
Intangible assets, net	823,280	682,977
Other assets	35,121	20,121
	$11,788,986	$13,494,011
LIABILITIES AND STOCKHOLDERS' EQUITY		
Current liabilities:		
Accounts payable	$ 55,692	$ 83,392
Funds payable and amounts due to customers	586,651	1,159,952
Accrued expenses and other current liabilities	578,557	681,669
Deferred revenue and customer advances	81,940	128,964
Income taxes payable	182,095	464,418
Total current liabilities	1,484,935	2,518,395
Deferred tax liabilities, net	215,682	31,784
Other liabilities	40,388	39,200
Total liabilities	1,741,005	2,589,379
Commitments and Contingencies (Note 8)		
Stockholders' equity:		
Common Stock, $0.001 par value; 3,580,000 shares authorized; 1,404,183 and 1,368,512 shares outstanding	1,412	1,431
Additional paid-in capital	7,272,742	8,034,282
Unearned stock-based compensation	(45,540)	—
Treasury stock at cost, 7,531 and 62,250 shares	(274)	(1,669,428)
Retained earnings	2,716,511	3,842,150
Accumulated other comprehensive income	103,130	696,197
Total stockholders' equity	10,047,981	10,904,632
	$11,788,986	$13,494,011

The accompanying notes are an integral part of these consolidated financial statements.

eBay Inc.
CONSOLIDATED STATEMENT OF CASH FLOWS

	Year Ended December 31,		
	2004	2005	2006
	(In thousands)		
Cash flows from operating activities:			
Net income	$ 778,223	$1,082,043	$1,125,639
Adjustments:			
Provision for doubtful accounts and authorized credits	90,942	89,499	100,729
Provision for transaction losses	50,459	73,773	126,439
Depreciation and amortization	253,690	378,165	544,552
Stock-based compensation expense	5,832	31,772	317,410
Tax benefit on the exercise of stock options	261,983	267,142	148,565
Excess tax benefits from stock-based compensation	—	—	(92,371)
Deferred income taxes	28,652	91,690	(227,850)
Minority interests	6,122	49	4
Changes in assets and liabilities, net of acquisition effects:			
Accounts receivable	(105,540)	(151,993)	(169,750)
Funds receivable and customer accounts	(44,751)	(132,606)	(146,900)
Other current assets	(312,756)	(49,371)	(443,530)
Other non-current assets	(308)	(4,612)	10,126
Accounts payable	(33,975)	564	32,986
Funds payable and amounts due to customers	216,967	251,870	575,137
Accrued expenses and other liabilities	39,618	17,013	(31,026)
Deferred revenue and customer advances	20,061	3,646	47,859
Income taxes payable	30,096	61,247	329,772
Net cash provided by operating activities	1,285,315	2,009,891	2,247,791
Cash flows from investing activities:			
Purchases of property and equipment, net	(292,838)	(338,281)	(515,448)
Proceeds from sale of corporate aircraft	—	28,290	—
Purchases of investments	(1,754,808)	(1,324,353)	(583,263)
Maturities and sales of investments	1,079,548	1,928,539	1,380,227
Acquisitions, net of cash acquired	(1,036,476)	(2,732,230)	(45,505)
Other	(8,646)	(14,696)	(7,158)
Net cash (used in) provided by investing activities	(2,013,220)	(2,452,731)	228,853
Cash flows from financing activities:			
Proceeds from issuance of common stock, net	650,638	599,845	313,482
Repurchases of common stock	—	—	(1,666,540)
Excess tax benefits from stock-based compensation	—	—	92,371
Payment of headquarters facility lease obligation	—	(126,390)	—
Principal payments on long-term obligations	(2,969)	(1,849)	—
Net cash provided by (used in) financing activities	647,669	471,606	(1,260,687)
Effect of exchange rate changes on cash and cash equivalents	28,768	(45,231)	133,255
Net increase (decrease) in cash and cash equivalents	(51,468)	(16,465)	1,349,212
Cash and cash equivalents at beginning of period	1,381,513	1,330,045	1,313,580
Cash and cash equivalents at end of period	$1,330,045	$1,313,580	$2,662,792
Supplemental cash flow disclosures:			
Cash paid for interest	$ 8,234	$ 3,478	$ 5,916
Cash paid for income taxes	13,875	40,256	179,169
Non-cash investing and financing activities:			
Common stock options assumed pursuant to acquisition	—	107,862	—
Common stock issued for acquisition	—	1,262,674	18,436

The accompanying notes are an integral part of these consolidated financial statements.

NOTES

Chapter 4

1. H. Thomas Johnson and Robert S. Kaplan, *Relevance Lost: The Rise and Fall of Management Accounting* (Boston: Harvard Business School Press, 1991).

2. Nathan's Famous, Inc., Form 10-K, 2007. See "Notes to Consolidated Financial Statements—Note B, Item 2," F-9 and "Item 20," F-19.

3. Build-A-Bear Workshop, Inc., Form 10-K, 2006. See "Notes to Consolidated Financial Statements—Note (2) Item (n)," 48.

Chapter 5

1. IMAX Corporation, Form 10-K, 2006. See "Notes to Consolidated Financial Statements—Note 2 Item (d)," 78.

Chapter 8

1. Big Dog Holdings, Inc., Form 10-K, 2006. See "Notes to Consolidated Financial Statements—Note 1," F-13.

Chapter 9

1. Crocs, Inc., Form 10-K, 2006. See "Notes to Consolidated Financial Statements—Note 2," F-7.

Chapter 13

1. Ram Charan and Jerry Useem, "Why Companies Fail," *Fortune*, May 27, 2002, 50–62.

Chapter 28

1. Edward E. Lawler, Susan A. Mohrman, and Gerald E. Ledford, *Creating High Performance Organizations* (Los Angeles: Center for Effective Organizations, Marshall School of Business, University of Southern California, 1995).

Chapter 30

1. Bo Burlingham, *Small Giants: Companies That Choose to Be Great Instead of Big* (New York: Portfolio, 2005).

ACKNOWLEDGMENTS

We—Karen and Joe—have been working together for about ten years. Our partnership began with a chance meeting at a conference and evolved over time into co-ownership of our company, the Business Literacy Institute, and now into co-authorship of the *Financial Intelligence* series of books. Over the years, we have met, worked with, and shared experiences with many people who have had an impact on our thinking and our work. These books are a culmination of our education, of our work and management experiences, of our research, of our partnership, and of all we have learned from our work with thousands of employees, managers, and leaders.

Karen first met John while conducting research for her dissertation. He was, and still is, one of the preeminent experts on open-book management. We kept track of each other through the years and were always interested in each other's work. Karen was delighted when John wanted to be a part of this project. He has been an indispensable part of the team.

Many other people have helped make this book a reality. Among them:

- Bo Burlingham, an editor-at-large at *Inc.* magazine, coauthor (with Jack Stack) of the wonderful books *The Great Game of Business* and *A Stake in the Outcome*, and author of *Small Giants*. Bo graciously shared with us the research and writing on financial fraud that he and Joe had gathered for another project. He also connected us with a wonderful group of entrepreneurs to interview for this book.

- Joe Cornwell and Joe VanDenberg, founders of Setpoint. We're grateful for their belief in teaching everyone the financials, and for their tireless efforts in encouraging everyone at Setpoint to participate actively in the success of the company. We're glad they let us tell some Setpoint stories. We want to acknowledge other Setpoint owners: Brad Angus (CEO of Setpoint), Clark

Carlile, Steve Nuetzman, and Roger Thomas. We also want to acknowledge Machel Jackson, Reid Leland of Leanwerks, and all the Setpoint employees. If you are ever in Utah, you should visit Setpoint; the company's system works, and you'll see both financial intelligence and psychic ownership in action. We suspect you'll be surprised at the employees' depth of understanding of the business and their commitment to its success.

- The entrepreneurs who agreed to be interviewed for this book about their own financial experiences. The group includes Chip Conley, CEO of Joie de Vivre Hospitality; Gary Erickson, coleader of Clif Bar; Paul Saginaw and Ari Weinzweig, cofounders of Zingerman's; and Ed Zimmer, CEO of ECCO.

- Our clients at the Business Literacy Institute. Thanks to their commitment to business literacy, we have been able to help spread financial intelligence throughout many organizations. It's impossible to thank them all, but a few who helped us and cheered us on are Dan Leever, Michael Siegmund, Greg Bolingbroke and Gary St. Pierre of MacDermid Inc., Shellie Crandall of Brinks Inc., Mark Boitano and Seema Khan of Granite Construction, Richard O'Donnell and Jeff Detrick of GE, Lou Poole Mobley of Gulfstream, John DeBruyne of PGS, Michelle Peterson and Elissa Harrell at KCI, Ron Wangerin and Melinda Del Toro of ViaSat, Heather Ludwig and Beth Dawson of GMAC ResCap, and Winny Ho of The Enterprise University.

- Our colleagues at the Business Literacy Institute. Rochelle Martel is one of those unique financial professionals who is also a fantastic teacher. Cathy Ivancic and Jim Bado are also both experts in the field of financial education, with the added knowledge of organizations with employee stock ownership plans. Marty Lasker and Brad Orton round out our facilitator team with their financial and facilitation expertise. Sharon Maas's extensive knowledge of business literacy is felt in our customized content development, class facilitation, and communication activities. Stephanie Wexler is manager of client services; her professionalism keeps everything running smoothly. Judy Golove, manager of training development, ensures that all our training programs are of the highest quality. Sam Case conducted the interviews for this book, providing us with key data to share with you.

- Dave Merrill, the creative artist who illustrates our Money Maps. His ability to take our initial rough ideas and bring them to life is a true talent.

- Jacqueline Murphy and Brian Surette, our editor and assistant editor at Harvard Business Press. Thank you.

- Roberta Wolff, who generously gave us her time and energy with an outcome that delighted us all.

- And all the others who have helped us along the way, including Bonnie Andrus, Deborah Annes, Helen and Gene Berman, Kelin Gersick, Larry and Jewel Knight, Daniel Kutt, Michael Lee and the Main Graphics team, Don Mankin, Kimcee McAnally, Alan Miller, Annie Petros, Loren Roberts, Marlin Shelley, Brian Shore, and Mike Thompson. Our heartfelt thanks to all.

INDEX

ABOUT THE AUTHORS

Karen Berman, PhD, is founder, president, and co-owner of the Business Literacy Institute, a consulting firm offering customized training programs, Money Maps, keynotes, and other products and services designed to ensure that people in organizations understand how financial success is measured and how they make an impact. Karen has worked with dozens of companies, helping them create financial literacy programs that transform employees, managers, and leaders into business partners.

Joe Knight is co-owner of the Business Literacy Institute and co-owner of Setpoint Systems. He works as chief financial officer of Setpoint and as a facilitator and keynote speaker for the Business Literacy Institute, traveling to clients all over the world to teach them about finance. Joe, who holds a master's of business administration from the University of California at Berkeley, is a true believer in financial transparency and lives it every day at Setpoint.